AN EASY GUIDE TO THE SCIENTIFIC PROOF OF GOD

by

Thomas Wright

visit us at: www.authorsonline.co.uk

A Bright Pen Book

Text Copyright © Thomas Wright
Illustrations by © Jo Spaul
Cover design by © Jamie Day

All rights reserved. No part of this publication may be reproduced, stored in a retrieval system, or transmitted in any form or by any means, electronic, mechanical, photocopy, recording or otherwise, without prior written permission of the copyright owner. Nor can it be circulated in any form of binding or cover other than that in which it is published and without similar condition including this condition being imposed on a subsequent purchaser.

British Library Cataloguing Publication Data.
A catalogue record for this book is available from the British Library

ISBN 978-07552-1267-5

Authors OnLine Ltd
19 The Cinques
Gamlingay, Sandy
Bedfordshire SG19 3NU
England

This book is also available in e-book format, details of which are available at
www.authorsonline.co.uk

Why this *Easy Guide to the Scientific Proof of God*?

I wrote my *Scientific Proof of God* in book form rather than as a scientific paper in a Scientific Journal on account of my age (87), and the time (amounting sometimes to several years) that it takes to get a scientific paper accepted and published, that is normal for a piece of original research.

When I had completed the manuscript and my friends read it, the message came back that the amount of detail and references to statistics limited its likely value for leisure reading.

I felt that it was a pity as among general readers there is certainly a huge interest in the subject itself. I tried to cut out some of the detail, but I found this difficult to do without diluting the scientific argument for those readers who would want this untouched, in full.

Hence this *Easy Guide*, which is being published alongside the more detailed *Scientific Proof*. I hope, dear Reader, that you will find it a useful introduction to the subject and that it will help you, if you have not already done so, more easily to make what is certainly the most important decision of a lifetime - whether, in fact, there is a personal independent God in charge of the Universe, or not.

If you are one of those, like myself, who finds absolute certainty, based on Faith alone, difficult to achieve, you may find this *Easy Guide* especially helpful. I hope so.

Many who have been exposed to scientific thinking feel that Faith, alone, cannot provide the answer, and that the lack of a scientific proof, to date so far, casts doubt on a God being present in the Universe.

What these people overlook is that Science depends entirely on measurement. Ultimately, all measurement depends on one or more of the human senses (sight, touch, hearing, etc.), and these can, of course, only measure factors in the Physical Dimension of the Universe. But the presence of God is on a separate Spiritual Dimension, which does exist, but which can only be measured in isolated instances, where it reacts and produces measurable effects on the Physical Dimension. This was only discovered clearly in the 1940s: and this single discovery (measurable Telepathy, Clairvoyance and Psycho Kinesis) has tended to have been ignored by scientists generally as being unexplainable. More recently, other instances of this effect of Spirituality on the Physical Dimension have been discovered, showing that a separate Spirituality Dimension to the Universe does unarguably exist. Science must now get used to the fact that until now it has been completely blind to at least one segment of the Universe, which really does exist.

(The illustrations were provided by Jo Spaul, of Norwich, England; I am very grateful for all the trouble she took.)

The next question to be asked about this "Easy Guide", is why it is formatted in so-called "Plates"?

This has been done because the task of proving God has not been simple. So little scientifically is known about him, that, in addition to hypothesising God himself I have had to hypothesise a number of side issues as well, such as the presence of a Spirituality Dimension in addition to the Physical Dimension as we have pursued the logic of the search in total.

At the end, these separate hypotheses have all to be resolved before one gets to the actual proof of God, himself. In order to keep these side-issues separate, I separated the text into separate sectors, consisting where possible of a diagram or some brief notes, usually of a single page, which I have called "Plates", and I hope will help the reader to solve the individual side-issues in a way that avoids them getting muddled together in the reader's mind. Thus, generally speaking, one can, I hope, view the evidence more clearly.

The basic logic of my argument has been:

(1) I have hypothesised what I was looking for.... what really is God like? One observation that came out of this was that He is a Spiritual entity.

(2) Before proceeding further we looked at what evidence there is of a Spiritual Dimension, quite separate from the Physical Dimension, and its rules. There has now accumulated sufficient hard evidence to conclude that, despite doubts in the past, a separate Spiritual Dimension is now proven fact.

(3) I then looked at the four areas where we know the Spirituality Dimension through its interaction with the Physical Dimension (Extra-Sensory-Perception with Psycho-kinesis, Self-transcendence and the Bible Code).

(4) Finally the evidence of the Bible Code (See Journal of Statistical Science August 1994) initially showed promise of the Scientific Proof of God, strongly supported by scientists around the World. Jeffrey Satinover and another writer, Michael Drosnin both wrote books on the subject, but then, unexpectedly a hostile group of statisticitans (Journal Statistical Science May 1999) challenged the 1994 researchers & the scientists who had supported the Bible Code Research generally withdrew their support and the Bible Code Story tended to fade out.

(5) I personally at the time was conducting a life-long search for the proof of God. I looked at the Bible Code story in depth and found that the 1999 challenge was only based on the finding of faulty statistical method by the 1994

researchers and in no way destroyed the hypothesis of the original Hebrew research. Thus the 1999 challenge was in fact completely irrelevant.

(6) I, therefore, conducted a completely new piece of research which proves irrevocably that there is an independent personal God present in the Universe and explains the likely misconceptions of some people among us, non-believers or "doubters" until today, who I hope will now see the error of their ways!

ACKNOWLEDGEMENTS

A Book covering such a huge subject inevitably needed to rely on other publications for information. A special thank you is due to the following:

"The Holy Bible" – King James version
"The Reach of the Mind" – J.B. Rhine (Pelican, 1947)
"The World's Greatest Psychics and Mystics" – Margaret Nicholas (Octopus, 1986)
"The Truth of The Holy Bible" – Dr Jeffrey Satinover (Sedgwick and Jackson, 1997)
"The Bible Code" – Michael Drosnin (Orion, 1997)
"The God Gene" – Dean Hamer (Doubleday, 2004)

"An Easy Guide to the Scientific Proof of God"

Why do we need an "Easy Guide plus contents?"   **iii to v**
Introduction   **1 to 4**
Section 1 - Situations leading no to "The Scientific Proof of God" to which this booklet is the "Easy Guide")   **5 to 18**
    1.1 How I became a convinced Atheist
    (including Plate 1)
    1.2 Life goes on (Plates 2 and 3)
    1.3 My slight, but only slight, hiccup to my atheist beliefs
    1.4 The rest of World War 11
    1.5 The War is Over (Plate 4)
Section 2 - Planning the Search for a Scientific Proof Of God   **19 to 23**
    2.1 Plate 5 - Summary of Situations leading up to this Scientific Search
    2.2 Plate 6 - The Logic of this Search - what is God really like?
    2.3 Plate 7 - God's Job no.1 - The Creator
    2.4 Plate 8 - God's Job no.2 - Manager
    2.5 Plate 9 - Hypothesising God's Plan when He first produced Man
Section 3 - The Spirituality Dimension   **24 to 37**
    3.1 Plate 10 - Hypothesis that God exists in Spirituality Dimension
    3.2 Plate 11 - Promising Area 1 - Practical Observations of the Paranormal
    3.3 Plate 12 - Promising Area 2 - The scientifically Proven Paranormal
    3.4 Plate 13 - Promising Area 3 - Self-transcendence
             - Promising Area 4 - The Torah/Bible Code
    3.5   - Text describing progress so far
    3.6 Plate 14 - The Wright family
    3.7 Plate 15 - Summary of Progress
Section 4 - The Torah/Bible Code - It's vindication - Proof at last   **39 to 48**
    4.1 Plate 16 - Proof of God, A 50 year search
    4.2 Plate 17 - Discovery of the Torah/Bible Code
    4.3 Plate 18 - The Story of The Torah/Bible Code
    4.4 Plate 19 - Extraordinary Predictions of the TB Code
    4.5 Plate 20 - The ELS Coding System
    4.6 Plate 21 - The Torah/Bible Code, False Challenge 1999
    4.7 Plate 22 - The Torah/Bible Code, My challenge to the false challenge
    4.8 Plate 23 - My challenge in 2010
    4.9 Plate 24 - The Results of my research
    4.10 Plate 25 - The Logic of my New approach
Section 5- What else does the Bible Code Teach?   **49 to 60**
    5.1 Plate 26- The 7 days Creation
    5.2 Plate 27- The Garden of Eden

5.3 Plate 28- Adam and Eve in the Garden
5.4 Plate 29- Noah and the Flood
5.5 Plate 30- The Flood Recedes
5.6 Plate 31- The Birth of the Hebrew Nation
5.7 Plate 32- Abraham and the Hebrew, plus other religions
5.9 Plate 33- Joseph offers a home to the Hebrews in Egypt
5.10 Plate 34- They Multiply in Egypt
5.11 Plate 35- Moses in the Bullrushes is saved
5.12 Plate 36 - Journey to the Promised Land Section

Section 6- Summary and Conclusions of our Search   61 to 64

6.1 Plate 37- summary of findings of our Search
6.2 Plate 38- summary of our Search (continued)
6.4 Plate 39- The Bible Code challenge is Dead, The Torah is a true historical story and is reconciled with the scientific story of the Creation.
6.5 Plate 40- The desperate need for more research into the Spirituality Dimension, to which these two books will, if successful, hope to provide substantial support

Appendix A   65 to 72

Results of my own research show that the Bible Code could not have occured by Chance

Appendix B   73 to 77

A bird's eye view of the Scientific Proof of God

Index   78 to 81

Introduction

THIS BOOK:
   1. **Is the Story, in abbreviated form, of my 60 years Search, alongside my normal career and family life, for** *The Scientific Proof of God*
   2. **It hypothesises the personality and working life of God, as seen by people who claim that they "know" Him by "FAITH".**
   3. **This, after 60 years of searching, led to a definition of 5 areas of human knowledge which seem to provide evidence of God's relationship with Humanity. These are:**
   (i) **Religious knowledge and Philosophy** - from when religions started however, little could be proven to scientific standards due to lack of scientifically provable evidence.
   (ii) **Observations, in practice, of Para-psychology** - (for example, Spiritual Healing, Prediction of the Future, Psychic Detective Work) - usually not replicable at will: cannot therefore be subjected to scientific proof. Some "happenings" happen so often, or are recorded in such detail, though that the thought that something "odd" is occurring cannot be ignored.
   (iii) **Scientific Proof of Para-psychological Events** - "Telepathy", "Clairvoyance" and "Psycho-kinesis". There is a large quantity of solid evidence, via experiments with hidden cards, dice-throwing and other experiments on these occurrences, that provide solid proof of their happening independently of the laws of the Physical Dimension.
   (iv) **"Self-transcendence"** is a proven characteristic of some, but not all, Human Beings possessed in their TCI (Temperament and Character Inventory) which enables them to "see outside themselves". Twin Tests show an inherited Characteristic which enables people to be sensitive to stimuli that are not of the Physical Dimension.
   (v) **The Torah/Bible Code:** my own personal research has shown that the first 5 books of the Bible (the Torah) contains, in Code, precise messages, including accurate predictions of happenings which are taking place today, over 3,000 years after the day that this part of the Bible, including these predictions, was composed. The coding occurs within the frontal text of the first five Books of the Christian Holy Bible, and Hebrew Bible (known to the Hebrews as the Torah).
   4. The total of the evidence of paragraph 3, subparagraphs (iii), (iv) and (v), above, which has all been proven to scientific standards; does show that **a Spirituality Dimension exists in the Universe**, which operates quite separately from the Physical Dimension, and does not obey the rules of the Physical Dimension.
   5. Sufficient research has now been completed on the Torah/Bible Code to show that it could only exist through deliberate insertion by a

Supermind, of the type which is only associated with the Mind of God. The Code was originally discovered by a little-known Hebrew Rabbi in the first few years after the end of World War II and the original research by a Hebrew team was published in the August 1994 edition of the *Journal of Statistical Science*. This research was challenged in the May 1999 edition of the same journal.

 6. I personally have challenged the 1999 Challenge to the Hebrew research via my own research programme, using new and independent data (in this book, plus in my more detailed publication, in *The Scientific Proof of God*).
My own analysis of the 1999 challenge (which was published, in the Journal of Statistical Science in May 1999) is set out in the follwing pages of this book. This analysis proves conclusively to scientific standards that Chance could not possibly have been the source of the Bible Code.

 7. I believe that the reason so little evidence is seen of God in the mass of scientific advances of recent years is that all Science ultimately depends on measurement by human beings of the Physical Dimension, using their Physical Senses of sight, hearing, taste, touch and smell. Anything that is outside the range of these 5 senses cannot become scientific data, except in those at present very few areas of the Universe where an activity in the Spiritual Dimension has a measurable "bounce-off" effect in the Physical Dimension which can be measured by the human physical senses. I think this is why, to many scientists, anything outside the range of the 5 Physical Senses does not exist.

AN OVERALL VIEW OF THE LOGIC OF THIS GUIDE
MY BACKGROUND

Position in early 1942 (my age 18)

(1) Church teaching becomes unable to make a mark on a population disillusioned by World War I	(2) So many bad things in world. If there were a God in the world, He would surely do something about them	(3) Science (i) thinking at the time presented an alternative to God being the Creator by offering an automatic predetermined Universe	(ii) science held the offer of so many benefits to mankind (iii) but no solid proof of God

I became an Atheist by the time I enlisted in the British Royal Navy in World War II at age 18

I had many experiences with people in war that tended to be spiritual. There was not much time to think about the philosophy of life.

Whilst in the Royal Navy I met and married the most beautiful, loving and lovely Welsh Wren, Hazel, The perfect Christian-by-Faith.

Married to Hazel I had no option but to live as a Christian despite my doubts. Due to my lack of ability to find "Faith", to satisfy myself I then began my search for the Scientific Proof of God. It helped me to find that many other Christians had doubts. The first stage was to find out what those who said they knew Him could say?

FIRSTLY I NEEDED TO DEFINE WHAT I WAS LOOKING FOR - WHAT IS GOD REALLY LIKE?

After a period of some 20 years, asking many, many people how each saw God, a constant picture began to emerge:
(1) God created the Universe
(2) God "manages" the Universe, day-to-day
(3) God created Man 40,000 years ago and now He wants Man to help Him manage the Universe, or the World within it.
(4) The Bible is a history of God's work
(5) He is a God of Love, Truth, Beauty
(6) God is Spiritual. He is all-powerful

Religion	Observed Parapyschology	Scientifically proven Parapsycholgy	Self-transcendence	Torah/Bible Code
Difficult if a person cannot find "Faith"	Plenty of experiences: but difficult to prove	Plenty of proof in "hidden card" and dice experiments in (1) Telepathy (2) Clairvoyance (3) Pyschokinesis	Recently discovered inherited characteristic of some people enables them to see "beyond themselves"	Discovery of masses of accurate and detailed predictions encoded in the Bible of events over 3000 years after predicted.

All 5 of these areas add to the conclusion that a Spirituality Dimension does exist in the Universe

The amount encoded in the first five books of the Bible is simply enormous. Human Beings could not possibly have inserted it. The two possibilities are:
    (1) The falling by "Chance" of the letters in Cover Text, or
    (2) Insertion by a personality with the capability which could only be that of a God

I HAVE PROVED IN MY TWIN BOOKS, THAT CHANCE COULD NOT POSSIBLY HAVE CREATED THE BIBLE CODE.

IT IS THUS FINALLY PROVEN THAT A REAL GOD REALLY DOES EXIST.

My best wishes to you, dear Reader,

Thomas Wright PhD BSc DMS FCMI FCIPD MCIM

SECTION 1 - SITUATIONS LEADING UP TO MY SEARCH FOR A SCIENTIFIC PROOF OF GOD

Situation 1.1: I had become a convinced Atheist by 1942

1.1.1 Disillusionment in Britain as result of Great War (World War I, 1914 to 1918

(1) Of the British population of some **40 million people** in 1914, around **7 million were men of military age**, including those unfit for military service and those needed on the "home front" to manage the country, **4 million either volunteered, or were called-up for military service** 1 million were killed during the 4 years of war, mainly fighting in the terrible war in the trenches of France and Belgium **A further 1 million were severely wounded** (losing perhaps a limb or mental faculties) This had an **enormous "disillusion effect"** on the whole population by 1918.

(2) My Mother (who lost a brother from tuberculosis caught in the trenches) and my Father (who had spent roughly a year in "the trenches"), although both brought up as Christians, never went to church after the war. My Mother made me go to Sunday School weekly. Her explanation: "You should learn about these things, so that you can make up your own mind about them later."

(3) At Boarding School (from age 13 to 16), half of my teachers had been severely wounded (one, for instance, had lost a leg; another could not move his jaw, so had to speak only with his lips - he was nick-named "Lipsie" by the schoolboys).

1.1.2 Decline of "empathy" with the Church

(1) At school, the normal Church of England services in the School Chapel were compulsory each day before lessons started, with two services on Sunday. The services all followed a set "drill", with the emphasis always on "obey".

(2) From age 13 there was no time put aside to learn about, or to explore or discuss, religion. All class time was devoted to concentration on passing exams in the accepted subjects.

(3) Prayer was compulsory throughout the school from 8.45 p.m. to 8.50 p.m. in all dormitories, kneeling at the foot of one's bed for the 5 minutes when the school bell sounded for prayers, and remaining there until it sounded the "all clear". Sermons in chapel tended to place emphasis on the rules to be obeyed in life.

(4) The main objective religion-wise in the school was that every boy should be "confirmed" as a member of the Church of England at the age of 16. Confirmation consisted of evening lessons in addition to normal "class preparation work" for the next day's schooling, during the 16th year of life. One had to learn the "Catechism", including the Ten Commandments, off by heart and to be able to recite them word for word, and at the final Confirmation service to promise to obey each individually.

(5) On top of all this, I personally felt as my 16th birthday approached, that I had to take a stand against the parrot-like learning of the Ten Commandments, which seemed to me fairly irrelevant, by heart for my confirmation, and I declined to do so. I was evicted from the confirmation classes. This approach to religion did not appeal to the emotions.

1.1.3   Preparation for the next war

(1)   The constant news (mainly newspapers) was of **military growth and preparation among other nations, and of international aggression**. The Hitler Youth movement was dominating Germany; Italy had invaded Ethiopia for no just reason; Japan was waging an illegal war on China. Germany was invading and conquering one free area of Europe after another - she had occupied the Rhineland which had been pledged as neutral after 1918 - she had occupied Austria, Sudetenland, the German-speaking part of Czechoslovakia - then Czechoslovakia itself – and, despite the German promise at the Treaty of Munich in 1938 not to do so, she had invaded Poland in 1939. This was the critical point at which we had to go to war for the second time in 25 years.

(2)   **The School tried to play its part in fostering peace**. A special effort made in 1938 was to try to cultivate a relationship with the Hitler Youth movement via an organisation called the "Anglo-German Bund". A group of Germans came to the school for a week; we played hockey against them, but they set the scene by marching on to the sports field singing the "Deutschland Uber Alles" German anthem as they marched to their individual places on the pitch. They were holding up their arms in the Nazi salute as they marched and sang and stood to attention in their places on the pitch until their master gave the military order to play the ball. At the end of an evening concert, it had been arranged that the two national anthems should be played. Whilst "God save the King" was playing, the Germans sat down firmly in response, continually spitting on the floor of our School Assembly Hall. Each of the Germans was equipped with a very expensive camera of the type which could only have been afforded for future military purposes to provide pictures for an invasion of Britain.

(3)   At school, we boys (fortunately as it turned out) underwent **compulsory military training** for two half-days each week. This included military exercises ending in firing our rifles on the local Bromeswell Rifle Range at targets which were replicas of German soldiers in their military gear, and bayonet drill against straw-filled sacks hanging from a frame.

(4)   All this atmosphere of war and conflict naturally **mitigated against constructive thought of a Loving God**.

1.1.4   The Influence of Science

(1)   Science learned at School had opened up the possible **concept of the whole world being an impersonal machine** in which everything that happened, happened automatically as a result of what had happened in the past, and what was to happen in the future was governed entirely by what was happening now, and that thus everything that happened was automatically predictable. This seemed to be a far more likely situation than for it all to have been created by a benevolent father-like God.

(2)   At age 16 I started my BSc course in Science at Reading University and **gradually developed as an Atheist** who believed in the science-based theory of Determinism as the way the Universe worked, as opposed to any religious theory of Creation by a God.

(3)   Science seemed to be capable of bringing about a **vast economic benefit** to society and thus enabled society to be able to afford social change. Although religion had paid lip-service to bettering people's "lots", it had not in 2,000 years been able to achieve much in this direction. Furthermore, there seemed to be no scientific evidence of the presence of God at all. If He is there, there would surely have been some solid evidence by now (i.e. 1930s to 40s).

(4)   The scientific theory of **Determinism does not need a God**, and could automatically go on for ever. If we want to improve the future that is predictable now, as we gain more power through science, we will be able to use this power to change things now so that we can thereby improve the future. This, with the lack of any evidence of a God from our all-seeing Science, means that there probably is not a God there at all. So = **THEORY OF DETERMINISM … THERE IS NO GOD.**

PLATE 1 - WHY WAS I AN ATHEIST?
[IN 1942 - AGE 18]

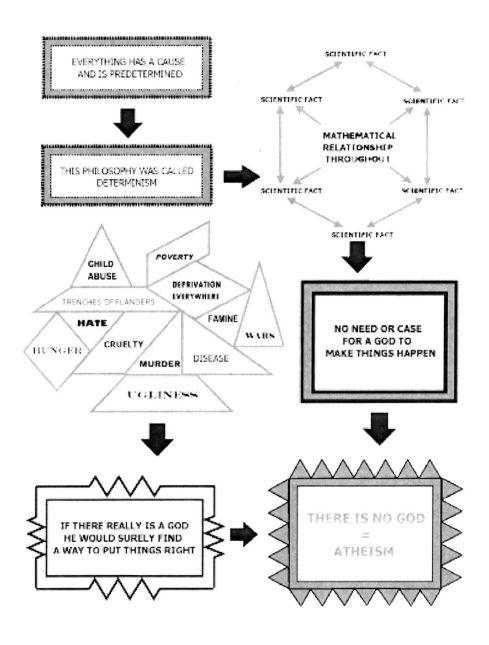

Situation 1.2   Life goes on

1.2.1   By 1942 I had completed two-thirds of my degree course at Reading University, the leading University in agriculture in those days. I had also reached the age of 18, when I would normally be due to register for military service. The influence of my scientific education had more and more confirmed my Atheism. The war had not gone well for us in those earlier years of our engagement in it, although we had, after the defiance we had shown in 1940 in preventing the intended invasion of our country by the Germans, avoided the fate of most of our European allies, that of surrender to, and occupation by, the Germans. The Americans were now, following Pearl Harbour, our active allies. The Union of Soviet Socialist Republics was now, also, our ally. Things were moving in our direction, but there was not yet room for optimism: what was needed was a real effort on our part to bring this about.

1.2.2   I, and my agricultural colleagues at university, had been declared as being in a "Reserved Occupation". Food supplies to Britain had been savaged by the German U-boat (submarine) attacks and resulting ship losses in the Atlantic and home food production had become an absolute wartime priority, so agricultural students were required to remain on their courses, rather than being called-up for military service.

This stimulated a lot of thinking among the agricultural students, as one could apply for de-reservation if one personally felt the need to join one's friends who were, more and more, putting their lives at risk to save our precious country. There were quite a number of us who emotionally felt we ought to be joining our friends in the battlefield.

1.2.3 So I, with a number of others, applied to be de-reserved. One other such student was David Irving, who was Company Sergeant Major of the University Senior Army Training Corps. David had the same problem as me, though ... he had become an atheist. We discussed this together ... What if we are wrong, and there is a God out there? Where does this leave us? We went together to see the University Padre - from memory I seem to remember his name was Rev. Sellars (unfairly nick-named "Soapy Sam") to seek his advice. "Well, I understand your position," he said. David put it to him bluntly, "If we do go, and end by not coming back, we just want to be sure that we have a passport to the right place, if we turn out to be wrong." The padre agreed with us. "I'll tell you what," he said. "If you tell me you accept Psalm 143 verse 10, and will learn it to the point where you can recite it as your understanding, I will offer you a private confirmation service, so that you are both confirmed members of the Church of England."

The verse we spoke together at that service was:

"Teach me to do the things that pleaseth thee, for thou art my God: let thy loving spirit lead me into the land of righteousness." We both had learned it by heart … just in case …

David and I met a year later when he was on leave from the 8th Army in the Middle East and I had come home from the Mediterranean to train for my commission. Over a coffee, David told me he did not expect to return when he had got back to his regiment: "I have a funny feeling that I will die in the water, with seaweed all around me," he said. "I can't understand it, though, because we are fighting in the desert, with no water anywhere" …

1.2.4 We both went back to our units: he back to his Scottish Regiment, and I to my ship. In due course, I later learned that he had, in fact, been killed. I learned after enquiring at the War Office that he had "gone under in a Landing Craft in the 8th Army Landings in Sicily" … So his premonition was correct! … even to the detail! … He had reached the rank of Major at age 21, I believe, which showed him for the soldier that he was. At least he had a ticket "to the right place"!

Situation 1.3 A slight, but only slight, hiccup to my Atheistic beliefs

In early 1943, I was at sea in an air/sea battle with German torpedo bombers whilst my ship, HMS *Atherstone*, was working on protecting convoys of merchant ships carrying supplies and support forces to the US First Army landings on the Western end of the North African coast, fighting the Germans under General Rommel, who were being driven westward by the British 8th Army under General Montgomery, who had been advancing from the Egyptian border.
One evening it was getting dark as we approached Algiers with our precious convoy. We were at "Action Stations", the highest state of readiness of a ship for battle, in anticipation of such an attack, when it happened. After two attacks from successive groups of aircraft, the third was coming in on us. I was an Ordinary Seaman gun crew. My job was to extract shells from a chute in the deck leading up from the ammunition store on the deck below, and pass these to the "loading number" for loading a continual stream of ammunition into the left-hand one of our forward twin 4-inch guns, so-called on account of the diameter of the shells which they fired. Whilst the guns were swinging round to meet an attack by a third batch of aircraft (from the left), my shell jammed in the chute. I was struggling to free it, but to no avail.

The gun had swung fast so that, unknown to me, it would be firing over my head as I struggled with my shell. I was caught in the blast and thrown by it against the gun shield that surrounded the gun emplacement to protect us from incoming bullets or shell splinters: I was rendered unconscious. When I came to, I was experiencing a situation which in these days of heart surgery has been known to occur to heart patients when their hearts stop during an operation. It is known as the "Near-Death Experience".

When I awoke from the shock of the blast, I found myself out of my body, sitting in a very brightly lit room, seemingly in a white cloud some 300 or 400 feet in the air above my ship. There was a tunnel with white cotton-wool-like walls and the brightest possible lights shining in the distance at the end of the tunnel. I was sitting quite independently of my body, but I was still conscious of it sprawled on the deck below and I could see the battle going on below me. Sitting beside me was what I can only describe as a formless "Presence", with whom I was having a quite normal conversation.

The "Presence" asked me if I would like to "stay" (presumably with him), or would I prefer to go back "down there", as he pointed to the ship below. I remember replying that I really thought I ought to go back, as I was very much looking forward to my agricultural career, after the war was over. "Oh, that's all right," he said; "if you go back, I was thinking, you might be able to do a little job for me, to help me, as well as yourself" ... I accepted this, and then he said "... but I would like you first to become a Christian, like you were brought up." I explained to him that I had gone to a lot of trouble over this issue and concluded that there was no God. I was an Atheist and I could not really change unless I had a proof of God to scientific standards, and still be able to remain true to myself and my friends. He seemed to be asking me this, to become a Christian, again and again. Always I gave him the same answer: "Sorry, but not without a scientific proof of a God really being there."

Eventually, I must have returned to my body as I woke up next morning in the ship's sick bay with the ship's doctor looking over me. Apart from being stone deaf, which remained with me for several weeks, I felt none the worse for wear, and the experience had seemed nothing very abnormal. I was soon back to my normal job again, manning my gun whilst at Action Stations, performing Gun Drill, "look-out" duties, swabbing decks and so forth.

The "Presence" seemed to remain with me, alongside me for several weeks, though, asking me again and again to become a Christian, "as I had been brought up". But always I gave the same answer - that I could not do so unless I had the proof to scientific standards that a God really did exist. In the end he came to me and said, "I'll tell you what - if you go home when all this is over, and live a normal Christian life, as you were brought up, despite your doubts, I will promise you that you will receive the scientific proof of God before you die. How's that?" I was puzzled by all this. I had "written-off" the whole experience as an hallucination and was getting a bit "fed-up" with all this pleading; so, without much thought, I accepted and agreed to follow his plan. The "Presence" seemed to leave me and I have heard nothing more from him since that point.

Attached is a pictorial representation of the experience as I remember it, that my illustrator for this *Easy Guide*, Jo Spaul, sketched for me.

At the time one was too busy to think out the solution to the problem of whether it would be necessary to comply with such a promise, made in desperation to a non-existent "Presence" or, indeed, how to do so to an hallucination, but at least I was no more being "troubled". Life went on as normal and I gave little further thought to the event in the ensuing years of the war. I was still a firmly convinced Atheist by complete conviction.

PLATE 2 - THE NEAR-DEATH EXPERIENCE (NDE) AT SEA [1943]

Self in white cloud above battle in discussion with "presence" with body still om deck of HMS Atherstone below

PLATE 3 - THE NDE ILLUSTRATION EXPLAINED

*I was a **Seaman in a British Navy DESTROYER** in the Mediterranean in 1943, AGE 19, in an air/sea battle. I was **blown up** and had the **NEAR-DEATH-EXPERIENCE**, similar to what has been experienced by quite a lot of hospital heart patients since the invention of heart surgery, when the heart has ceased to function midstream during a surgical operation.*

MY BODY WAS LEFT ON THE DECK OF THE SHIP, MY SPIRIT/MIND WAS 300 TO 400 FEET UP IN THE SKY, *above the battle.* **There I met a "PRESENCE".**

After some fairly casual conversation, he asked me if I would like to stay up there, or "go back" to my ship. I remember replying that I thought I ought to go back as I was looking forward very much to my intended farming career. He replied, "Oh, that's okay, 'cos I was thinking you might be able to do a job down there, to help me as well."

I recovered next day. **THE "PRESENCE" STAYED BESIDE ME WHILST I WAS DOING MY NORMAL WORK ABOUT SHIP (SWABBING DECKS, GUN DRILL, ETC) FOR ABOUT 3 WEEKS.** *He (or was it "she"?) was* **CONTINUALLY ASKING ME TO "BECOME A CHRISTIAN".**

BUT BEING A SCIENCE-BASED CONVINCED ATHEIST, I HAD TO DECLINE *(giving the reason).* **I FELT THAT I NEEDED A SCIENCE-BASED PROOF THAT A GOD REALLY WAS THERE, BEFORE I COULD REJECT MY CURRENT LOGIC FOR ATHEISM.**

Eventually, the "Presence" left me, saying **"I'LL TELL YOU WHAT ... IF YOU PROMISE ME THAT, DESPITE YOUR DOUBTS, YOU WILL LIVE AS A CHRISTIAN** *(the way you were brought up)* **WHEN YOU RETURN** *to your farming in England,* **I will promise you that YOU WILL HAVE THE SCIENTIFIC PROOF OF GOD BEFORE YOU DIE."**
His continual presence was a little disturbing, so with little thought I accepted and he left me. I have not seen him since.

Situation 1.4 The Rest of the War

1943 - I was sent home from HMS *Atherstone* for officer-training to be commissioned to become part of the massive Allied invasion of Europe by 1944 and, after training under Captain "Johnny" Walker in HMS *Woodcock*, one of his crack U-boat-killing 2nd Escort Group, I spent the rest of the war as deck officer and Navigator in two successive US-built Destroyer Escorts (known also as Frigates). These were HMS *Dakins* and HMS *Byron*, purchased from America under the Lease-Lend Agreement with the US. In *Dakins* we spent the early months of 1944 escorting US-built landing craft across the Atlantic in preparation for the invasion of Europe in June of that year. We then took part in the Normandy landings on D-Day (6th June) and on my 21st birthday (8th June) we came back to Sheerness to muster and escort our next batch of soldier-carrying merchant ships back to "the beaches". After that, we worked to protect the supply convoys crossing the English Channel, and later our subsequent landings along the Dutch coast, from the depredations of the fast fleet of German motor boats (so-called E-boats) that were working the North Sea against us. Eventually, *Dakins* fell to a floating mine that had been dumped in the sea in front of her on Christmas Day 1944 and she ended up returning to Harwich on one engine, switched to reverse. She had lost her bows, so could not travel front-first for fear of the effects of so doing, on the now-exposed forward internal bulkheads of the ship. For the remainder of the war, I served in HMS *Byron*, working from Glasgow and Liverpool to "clear up" the German U-boat fleet still operating in the Atlantic.

This job had now been made relatively easy by the successful decoding of the German Naval Codes with the newly designed computers working in Bletchley Park in Buckinghamshire, in the heart of the English countryside. We, for our part, were always amazed by the daily reports we received from the Admiralty of the exact position of every U-boat in the North Atlantic. We had no idea how they managed it! This had implications, as I learned later, in our search for God.
Only years later did we learn of the work of the computerised code-breakers at Bletchley, that saved so many of our lives. *Byron* was one of the ships accorded the honour of visiting the ports of Norway, after the Armistice was signed, to meet the brave freedom fighters of the Resistance movement there; before eventually taking part in the surrender of the U-boat fleet in Loch Erriboll, in Scotland, and returning our lease-lend boats to the US when the end of the war had arrived.
I have described the days of sea-service at war in some detail to show how little time there had been to philosophise further on such issues as the question of whether there was, in fact, a God "out there", or not.

After that, it was back to student life again after getting married, following meeting my lovely Hazel, my wonderful, Welsh, ex-Women's Royal Naval Service (a so-called "Wren"), 100% Christian-by-Faith wife for the next 60 years. From then on there was no doubt at all. She was such a wonderful example of the "perfect person", and of true Christian living, that I had no option but to forget my doubts and live as far as I could as a Christian.

Because I could not find within me the ability to "feel" the apparently blind "faith" that was all of her "being", I still needed my Scientific Proof, so felt that, to be honest with myself, I had to start my Search for the Scientific Proof of God that I had been promised.

After a time, my doubts were tempered by learning that many other Christians also had doubts. **I, myself, however, could never find the knowledge-by-faith that was her very essence and the pledge I had made in 1943 came back into my life. I began my Search for the Scientific Proof of God and continued it alongside my career and continuing happy family life. This *Easy Guide to the Proof of God* is the story of that 60-year Search.**

PLATE 4 - THE WAR WAS OVER

THE WAR IS OVER.
The Wedding (14th December, 1946) - a critical occasion

SECTION 2 - PLANNING THE SEARCH FOR THE PROOF OF GOD

PLATE 5 - SUMMARY OF SITUATIONS LEADING UP TO SCIENTIFIC SEARCH FOR GOD

At home	*At school*	*General*	*Science*
Christianity taken for granted, but not formally practised	Church of England teaching of religion seemed very "stuffy".	Life hugely influenced by wars, past and Present, and other evils. Surely if a God is there, He would have put these things right	(i) Seemed to have the capability to become of huge benefit to mankind (ii) Seemed to offer mankind the logic of a "No-God" Universe" (iii) A large amount of evidence about most things but very little evidence of God

1939 Left school to University (age 16)
decided there was no God and became **ATHEIST age 18 (1942)**

*I left University for **War Service 1942** -*
as Volunteer from a "Reserved" Occupation
because War situation looked so bad

Experiences of people and situations in war often had Spiritual component	*At end of war married to beautiful, lovely, strong-Christian-by-Faith Hazel.*

SCIENTIFIC SEARCH FOR GOD - UNABLE TO FIND "FAITH", *so needed Scientific Proof for my own peace of mind.*

PLATE 6 - LOGIC OF THIS SEARCH

In 1946, I decided I could not, with Hazel being the personification of God-by-Faith, itself, live other than as a Christian. **I decided, therefore, to live as a Christian,** *as I was brought up, despite my not feeling able to reconcile this with the logic of my scientific training, or find that miracle called "Faith". Any reticence I had about this was dispelled on finding that other Christians also had doubts. Not being able to feel Faith, I had to* **SEARCH FOR THE "SCIENTIFIC PROOF OF GOD".** *This book is the story of that 60-year Search alongside a scientific career and 60 years of very happy married and family life.*

My first task - to find out: What do people who know him, think God is like? What do we know about Him? What really are we looking for?

I hypothesised that a God is there. I then carried out a survey, asking those people I met in the 1950s and '60s, who seemed to believe firmly in God, how they saw him, I also studied the scientific information available to try to define who, or what, in fact, I was searching for. The conclusions were that:

THE JOB GOD IS DOING
(1) God = Creator of the Universe as we know it from Science
(2) God manages the Universe day-to-day
(3) God had created Man some 40,000 years ago, by mutating one single Ape into ONE SINGLE MAN, for him to multiply and help manage in the WAY HE WANTED IT MANAGED
(4) The Bible is the history of God's work as revealed to succeeding Generations of Man in words each understands

GOD'S PERSONAL QUALITIES
(5) God is a "being" of Love, Honesty, Truth and Beauty
(6) God is all-powerful
(7) God is a Spiritual God

PLATE 7: GOD'S JOB 1 - GOD THE CREATOR
There are almost certainly some areas Man does not yet have the knowledge to understand

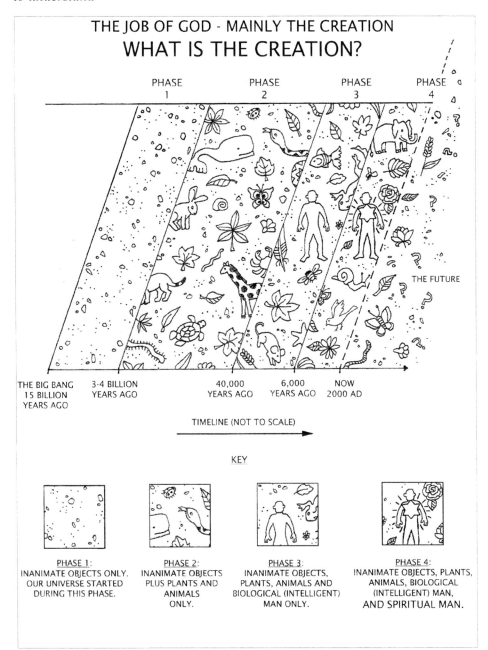

PLATE 8: GOD'S JOB 2 - GOD THE MANAGER

OUR ANALYSIS OF WHAT GOD IS, AS DEFINED BY OUR SURVEY OF THE VIEWS OF A LARGE SAMPLE OF THE PEOPLE WHO "KNOW GOD", NOT ONLY BELIEVE HE CREATED THE UNIVERSE, <u>BUT ALSO THAT HE MANAGES THE UNIVERSE ON A DAY-TO-DAY BASIS.</u>

<u>*The concept of modern Systematic (= Scientific) "Management" consists of:*</u>

(1) <u>Formulation of Strategy</u>: = What is our purpose -> Set Strategic Objectives

(2) <u>Organisation and Planning</u> = Break down Strategic objectives into Departmental objectives, which can be achieved separately, but in total, if achieved, must add up to achieving Strategic Objectives

(3) <u>Management-by-Objectives</u> = Regular measurement of Departmental Objectives achievement against plan in order to adjust management as needed from time to time, to keep organisation on course to achieve Strategic Objectives

God seems to prefer to employ Scientific Method, as known to man, so we hypothesise that He will prefer the methods of Systematic Management which are based on Scientific Logic

PLATE 9: -HYPOTHESISING GOD'S PLAN FOR MAN.- at the time when God first produced him?

1. Since God chose to use the natural method of Evolution, based on Mutation and Natural Selection to achieve His objective of getting Man into position to be able to help Him manage the World, we can hypothesise a <u>LONG-TERM PLAN. SAY 40,000 YEARS OR MORE</u>

2. From the initial mutation, then it evidently took from 40,000BC until about 5000BC to enable <u>BIOLOGICAL MAN TO DEVELOP HIS NEW-FOUND INTELLECT TO HAVING THE TECHNICAL SKILL AND TO ACHIEVE SUFFICIENT NUMBERS TO HELP GOD MANAGE THE WORLD.</u>

3. <u>AS MANAGER GOD WOULD BY 5000BC, EMPLOYING NORMAL MANAGEMENT PRACTICE, HAVE NEEDED TO UNDERTAKE A SWOT ANALYSIS</u> of the Strengths & Weaknesses, Opportunities and Threats facing Him so that He could adjust His Plan as necessary. His main weakness would have been seen as, "Man's lack of ability to communicate with God".

4. From this we can hypothesise that He would have concluded that with the Strengths, Weaknesses, Opportunities and Threats of the tools available to Him, He would have needed to:
(1) <u>TEACH MAN ABOUT GOD AND GOD'S REQUIREMENTS OF MAN</u>, and...
(2) <u>INTRODUCE A SECOND MUTATION IN MAN</u> to enable Man to communicate with God more easily on His Spirituality Dimension.

5. A historical examination of the Bible which we regard as hypothetically a true historical account, (subject to the explanations later in this book) confirms, of course, that these were <u>EXACTLY THE TWO LINES OF ACTION GOD DID TAKE. SOME 6,000 YEARS AGO,</u> in around 4,000BC. when He
(1), <u>INTRODUCED THE RELIGIONS, ESTABLISHED HIS CHOSEN RACE (The Hebrews), CREATED THE BIBLE, NOMINATED HIS INSTRUCTORS</u> (Inspired Humans) and <u>VISITED THE WORLD HIMSELF</u> (Jesus and The Holy Spirit)
(2) <u>INTRODUCED THE SECOND MUTATION</u> of Mankind via Adam (who, we are told was created "in God's own image") in the Garden Of Eden. Since Mutation would start from only one Man, Scientific evidence might not be available even after 6,000 years of development.

6. At this stage we are hypothesising the hypothetical track record of a hypothetical God <u>IF WE PROVE THAT GOD DOES EXIST, WE WILL NEED TO TREAT THIS PREDICTION SERIOUSLY.</u> Research will be needed to confirm the correctness, or otherwise of this hypothetical track record.

SECTION 3 - THE SPIRITUALITY DIMENSION (4 AREAS FOR SEARCH)

PLATE 10 - HYPOTHESIS THAT GOD EXISTS IN THE SPIRITUALITY DIMENSION (SEPARATE FROM PHYSICAL LAWS), LEADING TO THE PROMISING AREAS FOR SEARCH FOUND IN THE 60 YEARS SEARCH

God is hypothesised as being a Spiritual entity. The following areas have been identified as spirituality-based in our 60 years Search:-

1. PARANORMAL EVENTS WHICH HAVE BEEN OBSERVED TO HAPPEN, TO A DEGREE THAT CANNOT BE IGNORED, BUT WHICH CANNOT BE PROVED SCIENTIFICALLY TO HAVE HAPPENED. *This seems usually to be due to their not being repeatable for scientific testing. Examples are "spiritual healing" and "true predictions of future events"*

2. ASPECTS OF THE PARANORMAL (= spiritual) WHICH HAVE BEEN SCIENTIFICALLY PROVEN TO HAVE OCCURRED *and can be measured, but have not, so far, been explained by Science:*
(i) TELEPATHY - (the transfer of thought between humans without use of the physical senses) does occur (many hidden card experiments)
(ii) CLAIRVOYANCE - (the observation of events at great distances without the use of the physical senses) has been scientifically shown to occur in many, many scientific experiments)
(iii) PSYCHO-KINESIS - (the ability to influence Matter by the Mind alone, entirely independent of the physical senses) has been shown to occur (many experiments with dice)

3. INHERITED CHARACTERISTIC OF SELF-TRANSCENDENCE, *a recently discovered characteristic possessed to a degree by some and in full by a few [possibly 1 in 3,000(+)] human beings in their genes, enabling them to visualise situations beyond the limits of the physical existence (work of Cloninger of Washington Medical School, and others)*

4. DISCOVERY OF THE TORAH/BIBLE CODE *over years 1946 to 2010. We now **know** that the first five Books of the Bible contain a mass of accurate encodings of detailed predictions of events happening up to 3,500 years after these books were composed. The question is "who or what initiated or inserted these encodings?"*

PLATE 11 - PROMISING AREA (1) - THERE HAVE BEEN MANY PRACTICAL OBSERVATIONS OF THE PARANORMAL

There are literally hundreds of tales in human experience of "odd" things happening in relation to individuals that are quite unexplainable. Usually they cannot be replicated, so cannot be studied scientifically.

In the light of all this evidence, though, can we still pretend that the Spiritual world simply "does not exist"?

PLATE 12 - PROMISING AREA (2) -
THE SCIENTIFICALLY PROVEN PARANORMAL
(= proven by valid scientific experiment to have taken place)

MANY SCIENTISTS BEHAVE AS IF THE SPIRITUAL WORLD DOES NOT EXIST ...

And yet ... (see Reach of the Mind, *by J. B. Rhine, Duke University, and other reliable material)*

HUNDREDS OF EXPERIMENTS HAVE SHOWN THAT THE TRANSFER OF THOUGHTS BETWEEN MINDS, COMPLETELY INDEPENDENTLY OF PHYSICAL CONTACT, DOES OCCUR *(Thought <u>can</u> be transferred from one person's mind to another without the use of the physical senses)*

TELEPATHY DOES HAPPEN

MANY SCIENTIFICALLY VALID EXPERIMENTS HAVE SHOWN THAT OBSERVATION OF ITEMS OF THE PHYSICAL WORLD QUITE INDEPENDENTLY OF THE PHYSICAL SENSES DOES OCCUR *(some of us, at least, <u>can</u> see things at a distance without the use of the eyes)*

CLAIRVOYANCE DOES HAPPEN

EXPERIMENTS HAVE SHOWN THAT THE PHYSICAL POSITIONING OF MATTER BY THE MIND ALONE, WITHOUT ANY PHYSICAL CONTACT WHATSOEVER (= PSYCHO-KINESIS), DOES OCCUR *(The Mind <u>can</u> influence the fall of rolling dice)*

PSYCHO-KINESIS DOES HAPPEN

THERE IS, MOREOVER, AMPLE EVIDENCE TO SUGGEST THAT ALL THREE OF THESE ABILITIES, PRESENT ESPECIALLY IN SOME PEOPLE, DO OCCUR -
 - INDEPENDENTLY OF THE LAWS OF PHYSICAL SCIENCE *(such as Speed of Light, Speed of Sound and Operation of Gravity)*

PLATE 13 PROMISING AREA (3) - SELF-TRANSCENDANCE THIS NEW DISCOVERY (AROUND 2000AD) IS OF A CHARACTERISTIC IN HUMAN BEINGS, WHICH AT PRESENT ONLY A FEW HUMANS POSSESS TO A RECOGNISABLE DEGREE, WHICH IS A PART OF THE HUMAN TEMPERAMENT AND CHARACTER INVENTORY (KNOWN TO PSYCHOLOGISTS AS TCI)

1. IT IS BASED ON THREE RECOGNISED SUB-CHARACTERISTICS:
(I) SELF-FORGETFULNESS (= "LAST IN THOUGHT")
(II) TRANSPERSONAL IDENTIFICATION (= COMPLETE IDENTIFICATION WITH NATURE)
(III) MYSTICISM (E.G., EINSTEIN, JOSEPH SMITH FOUNDER OF THE MORMON RELIGION, GHANDI, SCHWEITZER)

2. IT HAS BEEN SHOWN BY TWIN TESTS TO BE INHERITED IN THE GENES)

3. A PERSON POSSESSING THIS CHARACTERISTIC IS MORE RECEPTIVE TO LEARNING ABOUT THINGS SPIRITUAL

4. AT PRESENT IT ONLY APPEARS TO BE A MAJOR CHARACTERISTIC OF ABOUT 1 PERSON IN 3000. SO IS PROBABLY A MUTATION OF THE LAST FEW THOUSAND YEARS

5. IF IT IS OF THE DOMINANT GENES, IT COULD BE VERY IMPORTANT TO THE FUTURE DEVELOPMENT OF MANKIND

6. MOST OF THE RESEARCH ON THIS HAS BEEN BY CLONINGER OF WASHINGTON MEDICAL SCHOOL

7. PROMISING AREA (4) - THE TORAH/BIBLE CODE
THE TORAH/BIBLE CODE IS PROVEN TO BE PRESENT IN THE BIBLE AND HAS BEEN PROVEN WITHIN THESE TWO BOOKS, "THE SCIENTIFIC PROOF OF GOD" AND THIS "EASY GUIDE", NOT TO HAVE BEEN CREATED BY PHYSICAL MEANS. THIS THUS PROVIDES THE STRONGEST EVIDENCE OF THE EXISTENCE OF A SPIRITUALITY DIMENSION. (SEE PLATE 19 AND THE WHOLE OF SECTION 5 IN THIS BOOK).

PROGRESS S0 FAR

1. My younger life till 1946 (age 23)

We have now looked at the series of events that I experienced in my earlier fife, until I was 23 years of age, in 1946 when I started my Search for the Scientific Proof of God:

1.1 We have looked at my own personal development, whilst a student, as a scientist and atheist.

1.2 We have looked at my Near-Death Experience, as a sailor, in 1943, I dismissed this as an hallucination at the time, and still do to an extent. But I do sometimes wonder if this was not really a genuine spiritual experience of a nature which we humans, do not yet quite understand, rather than dismissing it merely as "beyond explanation".

1.3 I have described how, after World War II was over, I met my darling little-in-physical-size wife, Hazel, who was herself, such a Christian-by-Faith Spiritual Giant that there was really no option for someone such as myself who found Faith so impossible to grasp, but to try to live as a Christian alongside her.

1.4 For my own piece of mind, I felt the need to embark on a Search for the Scientific Proof of God to convince me personally that a God did and does exist in this wondrous/ cruel/mystifying/ full of love, yet full of hate, world and total universe" of which we understand so little.

2. My Search for the Scientific Proof of God

2.1 We have looked at the preparation work I have had to do to try to make a beginning to my Search.

2.2 Firstly, I had to hypothesise that these Christians-by-Faith do have a means of discovering a God who does really exist somewhere in the Universe and that FAITH is not just "wishful thinking", as is claimed by so many "people of science". This, in fact, was not so difficult. It was made easy by being married to and living day-by-day with a person with a mind so much greater than to be deluded by such notions as "wishful thinking", as was so often suggested by scientists, as the explanation of "Faith".

2.3 Eventually I stumbled on a possible explanation of some people's inability to "see" this God that seems to fit. When one thinks about science, how is it "special"? Well it is only really special because the knowledge we acquire from Science has been measured, and can be described in precise mathematical terms as the result of this measurement. So we "understand" scientific knowledge; therefore we can use it. But some knowledge we have comes from experience, some comes to us from trial and error through which, perhaps, we know that these non-scientific methods of acquiring knowledge do work. I learned my farming originally in this way and until the 20th century began, the great achievements in farming, such as the almost universal system of sound arable farming "Norfolk 4-course rotation of Crops", was learned in this way by arable farmers who came to grow up on their family's farms to eventual leadership in the farming industry with only non-scientific knowledge to guide them. So not all knowledge needs to come through science.

2.4 The lesson learned from this was that Science is probably in fact blind to some knowledge, merely because the tool for measurement on which it (science) ultimately depends is the ability of human beings to use the five physical senses of sight, hearing, taste, touch and smell, and has no means of measuring those observations such as beauty, love, hate, and Spirituality which do not respond directly to these five senses.

2.5 From this hypothesis, the idea grew that there is an area of the Universe, which we have called "Spirituality", or "the Spiritual Dimension", to which science is blind. Thus we can hypothetically treat the People who say they know God, as really knowing Him through them having some other taught or inherited tool of sensitivity, that others among us, including myself and probably other scientists, apparently are unaware. We have called this area, of which many of us seem unaware "Spirituality", or, to distinguish it from the Physical Dimension, in which most of us spend our lives, "the Spiritual Dimension".

3. The Initial 20-year Survey

3.1 From this point I was able to seek out the nature of the God for whom we are trying to prove existence, by a survey over a period of some 20 years (from 1946 to around 1966).1 was thus able to record the views of those who believed firmly that they knew God by Faith, as to the Job God performed in the Universe, and as to His personal qualities

3.3 The initial 20-year Survey - "What is this God like, that we are seeking?" -lasted over my spare time from family, and normal career for some 20 years, from 1946 to the early 1960's, led to six basic conclusions:

God's Jobs as these people saw it
    Creation of the Universe
    Day-by-day Management of the Universe
    He wants Man to help Him manage the World

God's Personal Qualities
    He is a God of Love, Truth, Honesty and Beauty
    God is all-powerful
    God is Spiritual - not subject to the Physical Laws

4. My eventual Search for Scientific Proof

4.1 As well as my survey of people who said they "knew" God, I also looked at the whole field of human knowledge, known from people's experiences and from the accumulated field of science. After a total Search of some 60 years (1946 to 2006) I found in it my proof of God.

4.2 Examination of these key Job Areas and Observed Personal Qualities of the God that these people knew, led me to His likely future Plan for the Management of Man

4.3 Since my survey had found that the people who knew God believed that He lived in the Spirituality area, my task was to examine this area to assess the most likely places within that area, in which we might find God.

I found, over a 60-year period, 5 such areas:

    1. Religion
    2. Observed Parapsychology
    3. Areas of Parapsychology which have been recognised by scientific evidence: (in great depth infact)
    Telepathy   Clairvoyance   Psycho-kinesis
    4. Self-transcendence (a 21st Century discovery)
    5. The Torah/Bible Code

4.4. The evidence of all five of these, together, in particular (3), (4) and (5), are sufficient to prove that a Dimension of Spirituality exists in the Universe, which is quite separate from the physical Dimension and normally works independently of the rules/laws of the Physical Dimension. Area 3 is very important since it was explored in great depth in the 1940's and 1950's, but has been largely ignored by science due to prejudice (see the book "Reach of the Mind" by J B Rhine of Duke University).

5. The Ultimate Scientific Proof

5.1 We have also discovered that the findings of the Torah/Bible Code show an area of interface between the Code's source in the Spirituality Dimension and the Physical Dimension itself, (i.e. the physical Bible) where the results of its activity can be measured, and thereby the activity in this Spirituality Area can be proven to have taken place.

5.2 Despite a challenge to the earliest research into the likely source of this activity (the Bible Code), we are now, as a result of my own personal research able to prove conclusively that this activity was the result of an intellectual activity that could only possibly have been initiated and executed through a Supermind of the nature we normally associate with God. My own research proved conclusively that, despite the hiccough of the 1999 scientific challenge, which proved to be of no consequence, this Torah/Bible Code could not possibly have been created other than by God. God is therefore proven to be active and operating within the Universe.

5.3 This logic, which leads to the Scientific Proof of God, also provides Proof of other spiritual observations beyond the actual Proof of God. Supporting evidence of these other related Proofs leads to a strengthening of all of these proofs collectively

5.4 This research, which proves the existence of a Spirituality Dimension within the Universe also opens the door to the desperate need for research to try to find out more about:
(1)The Spirituality Dimension itself, which would be of entirely unknown size
(2)Any other possible dimensions that may be co-existing with the physical dimension. (might it be possible, for instance to find a way of measuring the relationship between the different colours, or of measuring emotions, such as love, hate, and anger?). It is intended that a large part of the author's share of the receipts of the sale of (a) the detailed book "The Scientific Proof of God" and (b) this "Easy Guide to the Scientific Proof of God", will be channelled towards a Charitable Fund to provide finance for research in this field.

By the late 1960's my Analysis of the views of God by those who "knew" him, had reached an end. I had completed that part of my career that was spent as an adviser on the scientific approach to agriculture, which had descended on traditional farming in England during World War II, and I was invited by U.K. government to set up a pilot plan in East Anglia for a government-sponsored National Agricultural Training Board under the UK Industrial Training Act of 1964. I digress from my spare-time Search at this point, to set the scene of my normal career and family private life, because I think this was largely responsible for the way I was thinking, whilst "looking for God". I was looking at the Job He does, rather than trying to imagine Him in the way we normally think of what his personality might look like or feel like, if He were in the Physical Dimension. We can now see that He is in reality of the Spirituality Dimension, to which our physical senses do not respond.

6. This Search was conducted on a spare-time basis alongside my family life and a normal career.

Firstly, Hazel turned out to be beyond any possible expectation on my part as the perfect person, and a lovely wife. We had acquired a lovely family and from my point of view, existence was a wonderful experience. I cannot resist inserting into this text, a photograph of our family, as it was (Plate 14) in the mid-sixties and which allowed me to be free to devote my spare time to the "Scientific Proof of God".

PLATE 14 - THE WRIGHT FAMILY AS THEY WERE IN 1964

I began my new job, setting up the new training structure to provide industrial training for the agricultural, horticultural industries in Britain, in the late 1960s. These industries were vital to Britain's economy at the time, and the job was well worth doing; we, as a country, were still recovering from World War II, and were still paying off our huge debt to the USA, which resulted from the wartime supplies we had received via Lease-Lend. In the 1960's and 70's any industry that helped us to be less dependent on imports was important indeed.

It was not long before we, in our pilot region of East Anglia, realised that the industry's main training need was in Management. I knew from my industrial experience that in the 1950s a new approach to management skills had developed in America. This had been piloted by a pre-war Jewish refugee from Germany, Peter Drucker, mostly via the Harvard Business School. Before the war, "Management" ability had been regarded as an inherited or inspired ability, rather than a "skill" that could be taught. Drucker showed that it could, like technical skills, be systematised into specific tasks which, in principle, could be taught.

I entered myself on a course that was being run by staff from Harvard. It was very quickly realised that what Drucker had done was to apply the logical thinking of Science to Management in the normal manner in which it was applied to the Chemical and Physical aspects of production, so far as he was able, whilst retaining those aspects of management which did not lend themselves to accurate measurement, as matters still of judgment. And this worked.

When we design a bridge, or a machine in the production process, for instance, we can calculate mathematically what materials to use, how much of them, and in what form they should be used. When we set about managing the production process, we cannot do this precisely because we do not have as complete a dossier of information on the factors being brought together in the Management process. What we can do, though, is to make comparisons between different areas of input into the management process, as we "judge" them to be. We can thus analyse any management job into its component parts.

We can then separate these component parts into three categories in the same way as we divided the physical process of building a bridge, or a machine. These component parts are:
(1) External Environment   -   individual tasks to be performed
(2) Internal Environment   -   individual tasks to be performed
(3) "Values"   -   individual tasks to be performed

We can then make a "judgment", based on such knowledge as we have, plus "experience", of each of the "tasks to be performed" and assign the judgment to it as to whether it represents a **S**trength, **W**eakness, **O**pportunity, or **T**hreat to the intended achievement of the Management (expressed as nearly as possible as one or more measurable management objectives). It is logical that if we **MAXIMISE the STRENGTHS AND OPPORTUNITIES and MINIMISE the WEAKNESSES AND THREATS in applying our management effort, we will be giving our efforts the greatest possible opportunity of achieving our objective(s).**

This Management analysis is called, based on the initial letters of the four words above, a **SWOT ANALYSIS.**

When we originally started asking the people whom we saw as hypothetically "knowing" God, we had not realised that their replies would reflect as "how they saw He did his job", rather than his physical make-up. These people saw Him as a Manager and person wishing to delegate his Authority to Man. His greatest Weakness was "the lack of willingness (rather than the ability) of Man" to carry out God's management job in the way God wanted Him to; God's greatest Strength towards overcoming this weakness was seen as his own all-powerfulness. This analysis pointed to a prediction of the management action He would need to take.

Without the application of that area of Systematic Management which had been borrowed from Science, we could not have been able to justify those predictions (of the role of the Adam-in-the-Garden-of-Eden, and the story of the introduction of religion into the world), that were made as a result of our survey of God, which, of course, are both recorded in the literature of the Bible, as having both taken place and have until now been ignored by science.

In the early 1970s I undertook a post-graduate course at the local Ipswich Further Education Institute, which is of University standing, by evening study over a three-year period and Management Training came to be the most essential need and need of all, in the UK farming industries. It kept me busy in the UK until the end of the 1970s. After that I started up my own firm of Management Consultants, working mainly overseas in a whole string of development projects in about 20 Developing Countries for the World Bank and other International Development Organisations from 1978 to 1999.

Whilst working on projects in the Middle East (Sultanate of Oman), many countries in Africa and in such countries as Pakistan, the Azores and Indonesia in the Far East, I was granted a PhD degree by the USA Pacific and Western University. This provided me with the confidence I needed in my Search for God, as well as in my every-day work.

7. The scientific research that led to a Spirituality Dimension

In around 1970 I quite accidentally stumbled across my first piece of science to provide really strong evidence of the existence of a Spirituality Dimension in the Universe which was entirely separate from the Physical Dimension - *The Reach of the Mind*, by J. B. Rhine. This was truly extraordinary.

I walked down to the village hall in Bromeswell to see Hazel, who was running the second-hand Book Stall at the Church Fete. To show willing, I was thumbing through the books she had on offer. There I found a second-hand, paperback book of the Pelican variety (part of the Penguin Book Empire) called *The Reach of the Mind*, by J. B. Rhine, at just one shilling (= 5 new pence). It turned out to be the story of the life-time devotion of a Professor of Psychology at Duke University in the USA in managing a whole University Department to produce absolutely piles of solidly scientific experimentation, all of which contributed, absolutely, to the scientific proof of the operation of:-

Telepathy - communication between different people's Minds independently of the physical senses, and independently of the laws of the Physical Dimension.
Clairvoyance - perception of physical objects at a distance, independently of the physical senses and physical laws.
Psycho-kinesis - control of physical objects without the use of the physical senses and independently of the laws of the Physical Dimension.

Rhine's work was conducted in the 1940s, and into the 1950s. To me, there were so many experiments and positive results, all conducted impeccably, that they proved unreservedly that a Spiritual Dimension does exist within the Universe quite separately from the Physical World, and is independent of its laws.

Rhine also bemoaned the reluctance of Science generally to recognise his work and that of anyone who dabbled in things of the non-physical world, even to the point of their careers being damaged by doing so, even if their "dabbling" in the non-physical world was only for a short period. They were often branded as "queer" because they had "dabbled in the spiritual". The trouble is that scientists will not believe that it might be traditional science that has the blind spot in respect of the Universe as a whole. So they have often tried to pretend that Spirituality and God just do not exist in the Universe, whatever the evidence.

To me, this was "the great find" after 24 years of hunting for a "chink of light" in the relationship between God and Science.

From then on I came across Self-transcendence, and the Torah/Bible Code, as further scientific evidence of the presence of a Spirituality Dimension in the Universe. The Torah/Bible Code research, published by the international journal *Statistical Science* in August 1994, was challenged by way of a further scientific paper published in the same journal in May 1999, but I am personally able to show through these two books, *The Scientific Proof of God*, and *The Easy Guide to the Scientific Proof of God*, that this challenge was without foundation and of no consequence in the wider scheme of things.

8. The ultimate proof of God

I have been able to show from an entirely fresh input of data, in my books, that it is certain that the Bible Code could not possibly have arisen by Chance. Therefore it could only have arisen as a result of having been inserted into the Torah Script by a "Supermind" of the nature that could only be associated with God.

This proved without doubt that:

A GOD DOES EXIST WITHIN THE UNIVERSE

We will now proceed to examine the Plates setting out the logic of the Torah/Bible Code as the Scientific Proof of God, and the nature of the other aspects which are proven at the same time and the steps needing to be taken to find out more about the nature of God's presence among us.

Let us go back to the point where we had identified the areas of scientific proof and general observation, the four relatively limited sectors of management of the Universe that enabled us to conclude for certain that a Spirituality Dimension does exist. This leads us on to the discovery of the Torah/Bible Code, which provides us with the ultimate Scientific Proof of God.

PLATE 15 - SUMMARY OF OUR PROGRESS SO FAR:-

1. WE HAVE HYPOTHESISED THE JOB HE HAS DONE:— as seen by those who know Him by Faith - THE CREATION

2. WE HAVE HYPOTHESISED THE JOB HE IS CURRENTLY DOING:— as seen by these same people -DAY-TO-DAY MANAGEMENT OF WORLD

3. HIS LOVING AMBITION:— that the Man He has created will in future HELP HIM TO MANAGE THE WORLD

4. HE NORMALLY LIVES IN THE SPIRITUAL DIMENSION, NOT THE PHYSICAL

5. THE SPIRITUAL DIMENSION IS PROVEN TO EXIST BY:—
- The Scientific Proof of Extra-Sensory-Perception - ESP (Telepathy, Clairvoyance, Psycho-kinesis)
- The Scientific Proof of Self-Transcendence
- The existence of the Torah/Bible Code

6. WE CAN NOW PROVE THAT GOD, AND ONLY GOD COULD POSSIBLY HAVE CREATED THE BIBLE CODE

7. GOD, THEREFORE. IS PROVEN TO EXIST

8. SCIENCE CANNOT SEE HIM BECAUSE SCIENCE IS BLIND TO THE SPIRITUAL DIMENSION - all science depends on measurement by the human Physical Senses, which cannot measure the Spiritual Dimension.

9. SCIENTISTS WHO WISH TO KNOW GOD NEED TO REALISE THAT GOD'S OLD TESTAMENT MESSAGES TO US WERE COMPOSED DURING THE TIME OF IRON-AGE MAN AND NEED TO BE TRANSLATED. AN ANALYSIS OF THE STORIES OF THE OLD TESTAMENT ENABLES US TO COMPARE THESE WITH THE SCIENTIFIC VERSIONS. ALL BAR ONE STORY CAN BE RECONCILED. THE BIBLE USES A LOT OF "FIGURES OF SPEECH"(DELIBERATE CHANGE OF WORDS) AS WE DO IN "DAY OF THE ROMANS" TO GET THEM UNDERSTOOD BY THE HEBREWS, THESE WOULD NEVER HAVE UNDERSTOOD LONG PERIODS SUCH AS MILLIONS OF YEARS. THE BEST EXPLANATION OF ADAM AND EVE, IS THAT IT DESCRIBES A SECOND MUTATION OF MAN OF WHICH SCIENCE IS NOT YET AWARE AND IS TOO ARROGANT TO SEARCH.

SECTION 4 - TORAH/BIBLE CODE - ITS VINDICATION - PROOF AT LAST
PLATE 16 - LOOKING FOR PROOF OF GOD - A 50 YEAR SEARCH

SUMMARY SO FAR:
Task 1 - Twenty year survey of "Those who KNOW God" What is He like?

A. JOBS THAT HE DOES	B. HE IS "SPIRITUAL"	C. HE WANTS MAN TO HELP HIM TO MANAGE THE UNIVERSE
(1) He Created the Universe (2) He manages it day-to-day	as well as all-powerful and a God of Love, Truth and Beauty. We should prove a spirituality area exists and then define it	We need to define how He intends to manage and train Man to do this job

Task 2 - How would Scientific Man interpret these answers?

(i)	(ii)	(iii)	(iv)
(1) CREATION 4 stages - Inanimate Energy/ matter) (2) Biological Life (Plants, Animals, etc.) (3) Biological Man. (4) Spiritual Man.	MANAGEMENT God using Systematic Management. This has only been a science for about 50 years.	SPIRITUALITY see as **only being in those areas where the Spiritual reacts with the Physical to produce results that can be measured.** [(b), (c) and (d) below]	MAN to become God's helper. seen as the product of the mutation of one Ape to produce Biological Man 40000 years ago.

Task 3 - AFTER over 60 years search all areas, I found 4 likely segments where physical science interacts with the spiritual dimension:

(a)	(b)	(c)	(d)
Observable Parapsychology (cannot be measured but "cannot ignore visual evidence")	Scientific Parapsychology (Telepathy, Clairvoyance + Psycho-kinesis, many experiments to prove)	Self-transcendence (an inherited characteristic of humans) (Cloninger: Washington Medical School et al. "See" beyond oneself)	Discovery of the Torah/Bible Code = **masses of accurate and detailed predictions of world events**

(b)+(c)+(d) Provide strong proof to Scientific Standards that a Spirituality Dimension exists

Task 4 - DISCOVERY OF BIBLE CODE 1940 - 1994 = If we can prove that Supermind (= God) is the only possible source of this code, this = THE SCIENTIFIC PROOF OF GOD

PLATE 17 - LOOKING FOR THE PROOF OF GOD
- *an obscure Hebrew Rabbi found an extraordinary range of accurate and detailed predictions of the future of the World up to the present day, that were encoded into the Bible up to 3,500 years before they actually happened.*

SOURCE OF BIBLE CODE
These encodings could only have happened through 1 of 3 possible causes:
(1) due to the "Chance" landing of the letters of the Bible's Original Script.
(2) the apparently unexplainable ability of Man having encoded it. This has now been accepted as "not possible".
(3) the encoding having been inserted by a Supermind of the nature we call God.

PROOF OF SOURCE OF BIBLE CODE in 1994: *showed that the Code could only have been inserted by God. This would be proof that God exists. At this stage many books were written about it..*

CHALLENGE TO PROOF OF SOURCE OF BIBLE CODE *(in* Journal of Statistical Science, *May 1999). The 1994 Hebrew Research was challenged by another Group of Scientists in 1999.*

MY CHALLENGE TO THIS EARLY CHALLENGE *(My Twin Books of 2010) My new books prove the 1999 challenge is irrelevant. Its whole argument rests on faulty Input Data and in no way disproves the Bible Code researchers' original hypothesis, that the encoding could not arise by Chance.*

My new proof, in this book (2010), proves, on entirely new data, that:
(1) THE BIBLE CODE COULD NOT POSSIBLY HAVE ARISEN BY CHANCE
(2) THE BIBLE CODE CAN ONLY, THEREFORE, HAVE BEEN DEVISED AND INSERTED BY A SUPERMIND OF THE NATURE OF GOD

THIS PROVES, THUS, ABSOLUTELY, THAT GOD EXISTS WITHIN THE UNIVERSE

PLATE 18 - THE STORY OF THE TORAH/BIBLE CODE

We have examined the four areas of Science, identified in plate 16, as Promising Areas in which we might find God. Now, in the fourth of these areas, the Torah/Bible Code, we really do hit the jackpot. We thought He must be operating in other than the physical dimension because Science, being dependent entirely on measurement by the human physical senses, had steadfastly refused to provide us with knowledge of God. Now, though, with the revelation of the Torah/Bible Code, we have found a physically measurable happening in the Universe which we can prove must be the work of God.

THE ORTHODOX HEBREWS *have always believed that the first five books of the Hebrew and Christian Bible (Genesis, Exodus, Leviticus, Numbers, Deuteronomy) - known as "the Torah", was as below:-*
1. *composed by God, himself personally,*
2. **handed by God to the Hebrew race at Mount Sinai, via Moses, their leader, around 1500bc.**
3. *that the Torah was the literally truthful story of the early days of the creation in the Garden of Eden around 4000BC and its history to 1500BC.*
4. **the Hebrew Orthodox Jews also believed that the Torah "open text" contained encoded within it detailed predictions of events 3500 after composition of the Torah.**
5. **God also decreed that the Hebrews should learn by heart the letter content of the whole Torah,** *and should pass this on through their future generations.*

<u>**Up to today the Orthodox Hebrews have held strictly to these beliefs throughout the centuries.**</u>

PLATE 19 --EXTRAORDINARY PREDICTIONS OF THE T/B CODE

Hebrew Rabbi's have tried to unlock the Bible Code over the years. This was without success until a virtually unknown Rabbi Weissmandl did so in 20th Century AD, 3,500 years after the Torah was first handed to Man. He lived in Europe; after losing his whole family in the Holocaust, he escaped with his ideas to America at the end of World War II. In America he tried using a computer, similar to the one that was developed in England during the war to break the German War-Code ... ...it worked! He found stories and predictions, detailed and accurate, even to dates and people's names, of events up to the 20th century, 3500 years after the Torah was first composed Some typical examples are as follows:-

1. **The work of Einstein, the Scientist:** encoded words bunched in one single group: **EINSTEIN, SCIENCE, HE OVERTURNED PRESENT REALITY, A NEW AND EXCELLENT UNDERSTANDING, A BRAINY PERSON**
2. **First "Heavier-than-air" Flight:** **WRIGHT BROTHERS, AIRPLANE**
3. **Discovery of insulin to cure Diabetes:** **DIABETES, KETONES, PANCHREAS** and other relevant words
4. **Development of the disease Aids:** **DEATH IN THE BLOOD, FROM APES, IN THE FORM OF A VIRUS, ANNIHILATION,** and others.
5. There were stories of **World Wars, Holocaust, Gulf Wars, Space events**, and many others.

   All of these were in the form of the so-called **EQUIDISTANT LETTER-SEQUENCE (ELS) CODING SYSTEM.**

PLATE 20 - THE "ELS" CODING SYSTEM OF THE TORAH/BIBLE CODE (item 4 in Plate 15) - CONTAINS HUNDREDS OF PREDICTIONS OF THE MODERN WORLD, ENCODED WITHIN THE OPEN TEXT OF THE FIRST FIVE BOOKS OF THE BIBLE (called by the Hebrews, the TORAH) IN DETAIL AND WITH COMPLETE ACCURACY

These predictions appear as encoded Equidistant Letter Sequences (ELSs) encoded in the text of the first five Books of the Bible, in groups, each group of words telling a story.

An example of ELS Coding in an English script (as per section 9.5 in Chapter 9 of the script of The Scientific Proof of God) is illustrated below:

ORIGINAL TEXT
I can do Vera and Lee a favor. Tell them a treat in store and I may be landed by son, Bev. He requiring to be there six days earlier than expected.

Adapted original text (letters 10 per line)	Text after ELS encoded cluster of words recognised by computer
ICANDOVERA	(I) C A (N) D O (V) E R (A)
ANDLEEAFAV	A N (D) L E (E) A F A V
ORTELLTHEM	O R T E L L T H E M
ATREATINST	A T R E A T I N S T
OREANDIMAY	O R E A N D I {M}A Y
BELANDEDBY	B E L{A}N D E [D] B{Y}
SONBEVHERE	*S*[O]N B E[V] H E R[E]
QUIRINGTOB	Q U I [R]*I*N G T O B
ETHERESIXD	E T H E R E S I *X*D
AYSEARLIER	A Y S E A R L I E R
THANEXPECT	T H A N E X P E C T
ED	E D

HOW THE BIBLE CODING WORKS
Identified ELS words in above

Word	Spacing of ELS letters
INTEND	+ 11
(I)(N)(V)(A)(D)(E)	+ 3
[D][O][V][E][R]	+ 4
{M}{A}{Y}	+ 6
*S**I**X*	+ 14

Coded Message
INTEND INVADE DOVER MAY SIX

PLATE 21- THE T/BIBLE CODE - FALSE CHALLENGE (in 1999)

The decoding of an ELS message was not possible before the advent of computers, which were invented by the British and Americans during World War II to decode the German war-codes. After the war, computers enabled this lone Orthodox Hebrew Rabbi, Weissmandl, to decode and prove the presence of these accurate detailed predictions up to the 21st century in Bible Books known to have been composed some 3,500 years previously. Fantastic, but true!

Typical of an important encoded "message" is the list of the names of 26 of the plants which grew in the Garden of Eden (Plates 27/28 of this series).
The whole story was revealed to the public in a scientific paper in the Scientific Journal, Statistical Science, *in August 1994 by some scientists in Jerusalem, which seemed to prove that it would have been impossible for these encodings to have happened by "Chance". The complexities of the accurate forecasting they contained, and the actual encoding 3,500 years ago, when the Torah was composed, meant that no human being could have given rise to the Torah/Bible Code. From then on, therefore, it was taken for granted in most of the "thinking world" that the encoding must have been the direct result of insertion into the text by a Supermind of the nature that we normally associate with God. Between 1994 and 1999 many books were written about the Torah/Bible Code, revealing masses of extraordinary seeming-to-be-true predictions.*

Then, lo and behold, in May 1999 this whole paper, Statistical Science *August 1994, was torn to pieces by a "Challenge" from other scientists in the same Journal. So others, often employed in "high places", who had supported the original research, tended to withhold their support to avoid getting their fingers burned and the subject of the Torah/Bible Codes (as at 2010) has not been heard about much since 1999.*

My book, **The Scientific Proof of God,** *to which this Booklet is the* **Easy Guide,** *finds:*
1. That the 1999 Challenge found no evidence whatsoever that the encoding in the Torah could have been the result of Chance. All it succeeded in doing was to fault the Statistical Method used by the Israeli researchers and to conclude thereby that the 1994 work had no support. Nowhere in their Challenge are they able to conclude that Chance could have been the source of the Code.
2. From an entirely new set of Input Data, however, I have now proved irrevocably that the Torah/Bible Code could not possibly, in any circumstances, have occurred by Chance. (See Appendix A to this easy guide).

PLATE 22 - MY CHALLENGE TO THE FALSE CHALLENGE

ONLY 3 POSSIBLE SOURCES:-
(1) could It have been inserted in the text by a human being?
(2) all writings hold some encoding due to the letters in the "open text" having fallen "by Chance". Could this be the source?
(3) the Orthodox Hebrews believe that God, himself personally composed the Torah. Could God (He personally) have inserted these messages and predictions into the Torah?

It has been agreed that human beings could never have been the source. Some Israeli scientists published their research (Journal of Statistical Research, August 1994) in which they appeared to prove that the encoding could not possibly have happened by Chance. (Journal of Statistical Science, Aug.1994)

1994 TO MAY 1999: *From 1994 onwards the previously unthinkable was taken for granted that the source must have been a Supermind that could only be equated with God. Many books were written about the Torah/Bible Code, revealing masses of extraordinary seeming-to-be-true predictions.*

THE 1999 CHALLENGE: *A new research paper appeared in Statistical Science May 1999, challenging the 1994 research. The many influential people who had supported the Israeli work and not much has been heard of Bible Code since that time...*

MY CHALLENGE TO THE CHALLENGERS: I HAVE NOW SHOWN IN THESE TWO BOOKS THAT THE 1999 CHALLENGE WAS OF NO CONSEQUENCE AT ALL AND AM ABLE TO PROVIDE A FINAL PROOF THAT "CHANCE" COULD NOT HAVE BEEN THE CAUSE AND THAT GOD HIMSELF HAD CREATED THE CODE

PLATE 23 - MY CHALLENGE IN 2011.

I, Thomas Wright, am able to say in 2011 that I can counter the 1999 challenge. Their case rested entirely on faulty statistical method by the 1994 Israeli Team. Nowhere could the challengers show that "Chance" could possibly be the source of the Bible Codes. They therefore did not challenge that concept at all, even though the wording of their paper implied that they did. Now I offer my proof that the TORAH/BIBLE Code could not have been caused by "Chance". God, therefore is the proven source. THIS, THEN, IS THE "SCIENTIFIC PROOF OF GOD".

-MY OWN RESEARCH, WHICH IS DESCRIBED IN THE TEXT OF MY BOOK "THE SCIENTIFIC PROOF OF GOD", SHOWS SCIENTIFICALLY BEYOND ANY POSSIBLE DISPUTE, THAT THE TORAH BIBLE CODE COULD NOT HAVE HAPPENED "BY CHANCE".

The first point to be understood, is that the result of any situation being exposed to Chance, is not, repeat not, "just a muddle". This is best illustrated by the flick of a coin. If we toss a coin, we know that it will land either "heads" or "tails". We will also know that if it lands by chance, alone, it will land, according to the mathematical laws of statistics, 50% heads and 50% tails, or very close to those figures. Even the hugest "Chance" happenings, such as the falling of the 300805 letters of the Hebrew Alphabet of 22 different letters, if subjected to a "Chance" happening, are predictable by the mathematical rules of statistics.

What I have done is to compare the original version of the Torah, including the whole Bible Code of all sorts of letter lengths, as it was composed 3500 years ago, with a randomised version of exactly the same Torah.

This 2011 Chance version will embrace, subject to the laws of statistics, exactly the same numbers of ELS's of each letter-length as the original Torah would have done after the surface text was composed, but before any "insertions" were made to provide the total finally published encoded version.

PLATE 24 - RESULTS OF MY RESEARCH (SEE APPENDIX A)

I have compared samples of the "mix" of the different letter-length ELS's that will always occur in a "Chance" situation with the 300805 letters of the Hebrew alphabet of 22 letters, with the actual "mix" of ELSs that is present in the published Torah.

I selected at random as many ELS's as I could find in the originally composed version of the Torah, that fell between "4" and "over 8" letter lengths.

I selected at random samples of 12 individual ELS's of each of 4,5,6,7,8 and "over 8" letter-lengths. My selection method was approved by two prominent professional statisticians.

I MEASURED THE NUMBER OF ELS'S OF EACH LETTER-LENGTH CONTAINED WITHIN:

(a) the original composition of the Torah
(b) a randomised version of the original.

I then calculated the percentage that the original composition differed from the "Chance" version.

The results of these calculations are attached as Appendix A to this Easy Guide, and were summarised as follows:-

CATEGORY OF ELS's BY LETTER-LENGTH	PERCENTAGE NOT BY CHANCE
9 (+) - Letters	100%
8 - Letters	46.36%
7 - Letters	32.77%
6 - Letters	18.65%
5 - Letters	5.49%
4 - Letters	-2.03%

(The minus net figure of 4-letters ELS's would have been caused by letters of shorter-letter "Chance" ELS's being used by the encoder of the published version, to create the inserted longer-length ELS's which were needed to spell the words of the predictions.)

PLATE 25 - THE LOGIC OF MY NEW APROACH (to Proof of God)
This is expressed in the following six stages:

1. Some examples of these encoded groups of words are as follows:
(i)   The life and work of Einstein, the great scientist:
(ii) First heavier-than-air flight:
(iii) Discovery of Insulin to cure Diabetes:
(iv) Development of the disease AIDS:
   - and many, many others.

2. Orthodox Hebrews have always believed that:
(i)   God personally composed the Torah
(ii) He encoded it with accurate and detailed predictions of Man's future
(iii) He handed the Torah to Man, via Moses on Mount Sinai, 1500BC

3. This encoding has now been proven to be present. It has never been considered to have been within Man's capacity to have inserted this encoding, or to have made these predictions

4. The scientific logic outlined above confirms that the coding could only have occurred if:
either (i)   the letters had fallen into these positions <u>by "Chance"</u>
or   (ii) they had been inserted there <u>by a Supermind (= God)</u>

5. I (Thomas Wright, PhD Bsc, etc.) have now provided indisputable proof (Chapter 14 of **The Scientific Proof of God**, of which this book is **The Easy Guide**) that the ELSs needed to include the <u>whole of the individual ELSs encoded into the Torah could not have occurred by "Chance". IT IS PROVEN, THEREFORE, THAT THEY WERE INSERTED BY GOD.</u>

SECTION 5 - WHAT ELSE DOES THE BIBLE CODE TEACH US? (1) (Plates 26 to 36)

We have proved that God exists through proving that only a Supermind of the nature of God could have sourced the Torah/Bible code. This also means that God must certainly have composed the Torah part of the Bible personally, but also by implication (since God is a God of truth) that the Torah is literally a true description of the history of the Creation.

<u>The Biblical version can be reconciled comfortably with the scientific version of the same sequence of events when one allows for the use of the figures of speech needed for the Torah to be understood by its immediate target reader, the early Hebrew people. The most likely explanation of the story of the Garden of Eden is that this was the second mutation of man as described in this section, that has not yet produced evidence by which science would know of it.</u>

This reconciliation, if plausible, will not only confirm our conclusion (plate 25) that the Biblical Version of Genesis and the other 4 Books of the Torah are literally true, but in doing so will add strength to our two other (paragragh 1 above) truths. It will also strengthen the case for the Hypothesis of the Second Mutation to Man in the Garden of Eden (Plate 9).

THE MAIN STORIES IN THE BIBLICAL TORAH WHICH HAVE BEEN DISPUTED UNTIL NOW HAVE BEEN:

(1) The seven days "Creation"
(2) The Garden of Eden Story
(3) The Story of Noah and the Flood
(4) The Story of the Birth of the Hebrew Nation, starting with Israel and its development to the time of Moses
(5) The Story of Moses leading them out of slavery in Egypt.

Let us look at each of these in turn.

PLATE 26 THE "SEVEN DAYS CREATION" (Bible Story 1)

This could easily be the sort of Metaphoric Phraseology that it would have been essential for any author to use, to get any understanding at all from the people of 1500BC, who would normally never be thinking in times of longer than a week. The use of this language tool of the literally incorrect unit of time (such as is today used in "the days of the Romans", "the day of steam") is still (21st century) regarded by language specialists as an acceptable use of words, despite the "appearance of looseness".

Note: Dating of the events of the Old Testament
We are now away from regarding the Old Testament stories as fiction. We need, therefore, to put dates on the events described. In this book we have used the dates calculated by Rev. John Brown (1722 to 1787), a prolific Scottish scholar, which coincide with such other evidence as is available. These dates were apparently calculated from the various "clues" in the Biblical text, of which there are many.
(See John Brown's Bible copy in Bromeswell Church, Suffolk, England).

PLATE 27 - THE GARDEN OF EDEN (Bible Story 2)

This can easily be explained from the words of the Story itself.
At Eden, "God created Man in his own image".

We know from our survey (Plate 6 Item 3, above) that one of God's objectives was to get Man to help Him to run the world in the way He (God) wanted. Man's first mutation from Ape into Homo sapiens *around 40,000 years ago would have brought Man after a further 30,000 years, say 10,000 years ago, to the point of becoming able to do so intellectually, but Man's "will" would still be of an animal nature. One can envisage that this "biological man" might have been concentrating mainly on the selfish animal instinct of "survival of the fittest", rather than God's wishes. To overcome this, it would have been necessary for God to create a "New Man" - "in his own image" - who had the ability to communicate more directly with God, and thus be more willing to go "God's way". The standard scientific way of achieving this would have been via a Second Mutation of one man to Spiritual Man. According to the Genesis story of the Creation, this is what God did.*

THE NAME OF EACH OF 26 FRUITING PLANTS AND TREES IS ENCODED (with greater than Chance frequency) IN THE FRONTAL TEXT (Known by code breakers as Cypher Text) OF:
   GENESIS Chapter 1 verse 29   to   GENESIS Ch. 2 v. 16
   and GENESIS Ch. 2 v. 7   to   GENESIS Ch. 3 v. 3
   (in which the Open Text records the Story of the Garden of Eden)
The encoded plant names are - Barley, Wheat, Vine, Chestnut, Grape, Thicket, Date palm, Acacia, Boxthorn, Cedar, Willow, Pomegranate, Aloe, Oak, Gopher wood, Citron, Poplar, Terebinth, Thornbush, Cassia, Almond, Hazel, Olive, Pistaccio, Tamarisk and Fig.

It looks as if this encoding might have been God's way of giving his signature in proof of the reality of this event (Eden) . . . also of his authorship of this part of Genesis?

PLATE 28 - ADAM AND EVE IN THE GARDEN – (4000BC)

- *Were these the first human beings carrying genes for the development of a "New Man in the image of God?"*

It is noted that each one of the plants indicated above is separately encoded by ELS in the brief description of the Garden of Eden contained in the normally-read open-text parts of Genesis, Chapters 1, 2 and 3, describing the Garden. The likelihood of this encoding happening by chance is non-existent. It is noted that this list of plants embraces every possible human need, even a medical plant, cassia (= senna), which is still used to relieve constipation today!

Note the "star" on Adam, representing his new spiritual genes.

PLATE 29 - NOAH AND THE FLOOD (Bible Story 3)

The Bible Story tells us that God, only 1,500 years after Adam, decided that the New Man was not developing in the way He intended. He needed to remove the new mutation entirely, except for his chosen one and family, which is what the Bible tells us He did.

Use of the word "man" in Genesis always refers only to those who were descendants of Adam. It is fair to comment that Adam's stock would, with the limited transport and high death rates of those days (2500BC), not have occupied a large area in only 1,500 years since Eden. So it would not have been impossible for a flood to remove them all. Human disease, and crop and animal disease leading to famine, would follow such a flood and lead to multiple deaths as a result of such a flood.

The Story happened 1,000 years before composition date of the Torah and there was no pictorial record. The story of the First Five Books as told in Genesis was composed to be understood by people 3,500 years ago with limited understanding and limited communication capability; the composer had to describe it as briefly as possible. Some interpretation, on our part, is surely, therefore, justified ... and essential.

The story of the Torah/Bible Code, which the Orthodox Hebrews always believed to be true, has been judged by some "modern" people to be "quite impossible", but it has now been proven valid by the evidence provided in this book. It is surely not wise to dismiss another of their firm beliefs (the genesis "flood" story) without very careful consideration.

There is considerable circumstantial evidence (lava remains found today in the Nile Delta area, timing, nature and sequence of the plagues, etc.) that the events described in Genesis about the Hebrew Exodus from Egypt were a logical sequel and could have actually happened as a result of the massive volcanic eruption of the Greek island Santerini in around 1500BC. Computer simulation has shown that this would have started a tidal wave 600 feet high travelling at 400 miles per hour across the Mediterranean, giving rise to the very conditions described at the time the Hebrews were crossing the Nile, described in Genesis. Volcanic shards, thought to have come from Santorini, have been found in Egypt. (Reference BBC1 programme "Moses", 1st December 2002 and UK Daily Telegraph, page 5, 11.11.02).

If we searched seriously, it is not impossible that we might find evidence of the reality of Noah's Flood in due course.

PLATE 30 - THE FLOOD RECEDES(4)
- and the rainbow "takes over" (see the Bible story - Genesis, chapter 9, verses 12 to 17) ... 2347BC

PLATE 31 - THE BIRTH OF THE HEBREW NATION (5)

ABRAHAM
Born 1996BC	-	*2 years after death of Noah*
1921BC	-	*He entered into a **Covenant with God***
1896BC	-	***SARAH**, Abraham's wife, gives birth to **ISAAC***
	-	*Abraham had also fathered another son, **ISHMAEL**, by their maidservant Hagar*
1856BC	-	***ISAAC** marries **REBECCA***
1821BC	-	*Isaac and Rebecca have two sons: **JACOB** (later re-named **Israel**), and **ESAU***

ABRAHAM *fathered the Hebrew Nation through his grandson, Israel (formerly known as Jacob), via his son, Isaac, who was Jacob's father. It is claimed by the Arabs that he also fathered the Arab Nation through his other son, Ishmael.* **Importantly, therefore, Abraham is thus held in high esteem by all three great religions: Zionism, Christianity and Islam.**

ISRAEL (former name - Jacob)
By 1753BC has 11 sons and 1 daughter. 1728BC - JOSEPH, aged 17, is Israel's favourite son, and is given a Coat of Many Colours by his Father. In envy, the brothers secretly kidnapped and sold Joseph into slavery in Egypt.

THE HEBREWS IN EGYPT
1739BC - Joseph became a slave to Potiphar, ruler of Egypt under Pharoah. Later, after interpreting Pharoah's dreams correctly, **predicting** *7* **years of plenty followed by 7 years of famine, he was promoted to become ruler of all Egypt directly under Pharoah.**

As Prime Minister, he set aside food during the 7 years of plenty to feed the people over the ensuing drought. Pharoah was well pleased.
The Israelite brothers also suffered from the drought. Not being aware of the position to which Joseph had been raised, they came to Egypt to buy corn for themselves. The brothers did not recognise Joseph: it was 22 years since they sold and last saw him. In due course, Joseph made himself known to them, and invited the whole family of Israel to stay in Egypt to outstay the famine. His invitation was accepted.

PLATE 32 – ABRAHAM (6)

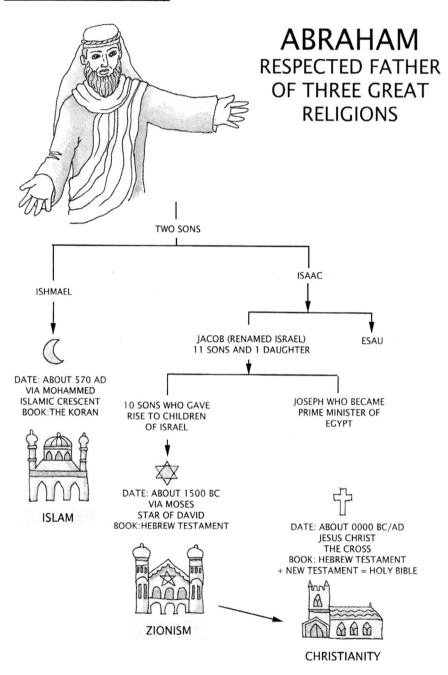

PLATE 33 - JOSEPH OFFERS THE HEBREWS A HOME IN EGYPT (7)

PLATE 34 - THEY MULTIPLY [IN EGYPT (8)]

The Israelite family (from Israel's 11 sons + 1 daughter) stayed in Egypt as free men and women for nearly 150 years. They multiplied so much that the Egyptians felt they had to suppress them (1591BC). To reduce population pressure, Pharoah instructed that all Hebrew baby boys were to be killed at birth.

During this time, Moses was born; his mother laid him on the riverside, hoping that he would be picked up and not be killed. He happened to be found by an Egyptian princess who arranged for him to be looked after and to receive an education.

Eventually, the Egyptians turned the Hebrews over to slavery. In 1491BC, God appeared to Moses from a burning bush and told him that, in conjunction with his brother Aaron, he was to lead the Children of Israel out of Egypt, into "The Wilderness", eventually to reach "the Promised Land", which was to be their home.

The Hebrews responded to Moses' leadership. They suffered from floods and plagues galore in their flight and eventually reached Mount Sinai. There is considerable circumstantial evidence (lava, timing, nature and sequence of ten plagues, etc.) to indicate that these events could have actually happened as the result of a massive volcanic eruption which took place on the Greek Island of Santerini. This exploded in the 15th/16th centuries BC, with a tidal wave 600ft high travelling at 400 mph across the Mediterranean. This evidence is purely circumstantial, but it could eventually lead to proof of the truth of the story.

It is held by the Orthodox Hebrews to this day that it was, at Sinai, 50 days after their escape from Egypt, that God, having himself composed it, passed the text of the current Torah (the first five Books of the Bible – Genesis, Exodus, Leviticus, Numbers, Deuteronomy) via Moses to the Hebrews, indicating that all future Hebrew priests were to be the direct descendants of Aaron, which they remain today. He instructed that they, the Hebrew rabbis, were to memorise the Torah on a letter-by-letter basis, and hand it on, together with the Jewish Law, down through the generations "till the end of days".

This they have done, and today every copy of the Torah in every Orthodox Synagogue in the world is spelt exactly alike, and contains the mysterious Torah/Bible Code. It is this version that, thanks to the brilliant Rabbi Weissmandl, and the World War II allies' discovery of the computer to aid code-breaking, that we are now able to read The Bible Code, which we now know God personally composed.

PLATE 35 - MOSES IS SAVED *(9) (from King Pharoah's decree that all male Hebrew babies should be killed. He was hidden in the bulrushes by his Mother, and later found by the Egyptian Princess. She arranged for him to be cared for and educated).*

PLATE 36 - JOURNEY TO THE "PROMISED LAND"

*40 years in the Wilderness led by Moses - between approx. 1500 to 1450BC - where they eventually established their "home" and grew to foster the two great religions of Judaism and Christianity, and all this means in the 21st century, now that <u>**we know by Scientific Reasoning as well as by Faith, that it is all, absolutely, The Truth.**</u>*

SECTION 6 - SUMMARY AND CONCLUSIONS

PLATE 37 - A SUMMARY OF FINDINGS OF OUR SEARCH (1)

*You, my readers, and I set out in this book to search for the Scientific Proof of God, which had been promised to me, in what **now appears to have been a Spiritual Experience**, but which I at the time regarded as an Hallucination, **in the early weeks of 1943, during the North African Landings of World War II.** That search is now complete and has covered the whole of the present range of Scientific Knowledge that is in 2011 available to mankind. The following is a summary:*

1. A HUGE VOLUME OF PARA-PSYCHOLOGICAL EXPERIENCES WHICH CANNOT BE PROVED SCIENTIFICALLY.

*I personally believe that so many of these para-psychological experiences occur (such as in psychic healing), and some (such as Uri Geller's spoon-bending and the finding of the Queen of England's "Coronation Stone" by a Dutch Psychic Detective), have been so vividly observed by so many that they must indicate that **something unusual happens outside the physical dimension.***

2. Secondly, we have **SCIENTIFIC EVIDENCE WHICH PROVES THE OPERATION OF THE PSI FACTOR**
   - (i) **TELEPATHY** *(= non-physical communication between minds)*
   - (ii) **CLAIRVOYANCE** *(= non-physical communication between mind and matter)*
   - (iii) **PSYCHO-KINESIS** *(= mind independently able to manipulate matter)*
   - (iv) They have all three been proven to take place by a huge volume of scientific experiments with cards and falling dice. There is strong evidence that **they operate independently of the rules of the physical dimension.**

3. Thirdly: Modern research has shown that:
   (i) some people possess the **unique inherited characteristic of SELF-TRANSCENDENCE**. This is based on three sub-characteristics:
   (a) **Self-forgetfulness** *(ability to get lost in one's own thoughts)*
   (b) **Transpersonal Identification** *(ability to "be as one" with nature)*
   (c) **Mysticism** *(such as possessed by Einstein, Ghandi and Joseph Smith, founder of the Mormon Church)*
   None of these three sub-characteristics is dependent on other than heritable factors (i.e. not dependant on un-inherited factors such as mental stress or anxiety).

PLATE 38 - SUMMARY OF OUR SEARCH (Continued from Plate 37) *(item 3, Self-transcendence)*

(ii) Self-transcendence has been proven by "twin tests" to be inherited.

(iii) Self-transcendence enables a person to be more receptive of religious teaching, but is not, itself, a religion. Each religion is, separately, a "taught skill".

(iv) Most of the research on this subject has been by Cloninger of Washington Medical School.

(v) Only a few individuals (some 1 in 3,000) seem to possess this characteristic in full at present.

(vi) Current evidence seems to point to a *fairly recent mutation in the genetic characteristic of mankind. This means that if it turns out to be a dominant mutation, IT COULD HAVE THE POTENTIAL TO CHANGE THE HUMAN RACE DRAMATICALLY, SPIRITUALLY, IN FUTURE GENERATIONS*

4. FOURTHLY, WE HAVE FOUND THE TORAH/BIBLE CODE.
The first five Books of the Bible are intricately encoded in ELS format, with accurate and detailed predictions of the future up to 3,500 years after these books were composed (e.g. World War II, the Holocaust, the discovery of Insulin to cure Diabetes, the onset of the disease Aids, the First Gulf War, and others, as well as details of other stories within those books (e.g Garden of Eden trees and plants).

It is recognised that this encoding is beyond the capability of current or previous Human Beings. It must, therefore, have been the result of either the encoded letters falling into place by "Chance" from their positions in the overall "Cypher Text", or from their having been put in place by a Supermind of the nature which we normally associate with God.

In this book so far, we have worked on the hypothesis that the encoding could not possibly have resulted by Chance, which seemed fairly obvious at first examination, it must, therefore, have been the result of God's work, when He composed the first five Books, as is categorically believed today by the Orthodox Hebrew Church. We have shown how the research, which was presented via the scientific journal, Statistical Science, *in May 1999, intending to challenge the Israeli research on the impossibility of it having arisen by Chance is now, from my own figures, proven to be invalid as a basis for this conclusion. My own figures now prove irrevocably that the Bible Code in the Torah could not have happened by chance (see Appendix A).*

PLATE 39 - THE BIBLE CODE CHALLENGE (Journal of Statistical Science, May 1999) IS DEAD. SO THE TORAH/BIBLE BIBLE CODE IS NOW VINDICATED.

I myself examined the position in detail and, as reported in my book The Scientific Proof of God, *concluded that the challenge was entirely based on the use of a faulty statistical method by the original Israeli researchers and in no way justified a conclusion that the Bible Code could possibly, in any circumstances, have occurred by Chance. I have explained my scientific reasoning that the 1999 challenge was invalid and set about taking an entirely new approach to prove indisputably that the Torah/Bible Code could not have occurred by Chance. This having been proved, the Code must have been inserted. There is no one capable, of executing this insertion, other than a Supermind of the calibre we normally associate with God; it is thus **proven that a GOD, THEREFORE, EXISTS.** The fact that the Torah/Bible Code has been proven to have been inserted by God also confirms another "truth" that is also a firm belief of the Orthodox Hebrew Church, i.e. that the **TORAH IS A LITERAL TRUE HISTORICAL DOCUMENT.** We found that **THE TWO VERSIONS OF THE HISTORY OF THE CREATION OF MAN (BIBLICAL AND SCIENTIFIC) ARE SURPRISINGLY RECONCILABLE**.*

We also found that the evidence is building up to support these 3 conclusions (through, for example, projections of the volcanic explosion of the Greek Island of Santerini in around 1500BC).

*It seems probable that the only difference between the text of the Bible and the Scientific version lies in such areas as the use of figures of speech and metaphorical wording, of the type regarded as normal in any text to overcome such problems as the limited understanding abilities of the original target population to whom the text was being addressed. It is also quite understandable that Science has not yet latched on to the biological mutation of a "new Spiritual Man" only some 6,000 years ago, but scientific evidence of a gradually increasing inherited effect of this one-man mutation is gradually accumulating. It is noted that the last major one-unit mutation recognised by science (from Ape to Biological Man) has taken 40,000 years at compound interest rate to reach its present universality. It is noted that a biological mutation multiplies in "geometric progression" from a single animal or plant. This means relatively small increases in numbers during the early centuries of its existence. **More research on this is very much needed.***

PLATE 40 - THE DESPERATE NEED FOR MORE RESEARCH

Science has tended to regard anything bordering on Spirituality as not being a suitable area in which to invest time and money.

This must be put right.

We now urgently need to research the following areas:
  1. **Reconciliation of Scientific and Biblical views of the Creation.**
  2. **Is Spirituality a characteristic that anyone can acquire through teaching**, *as most people of religion believe, or does it have a hereditary component, as seems to be suggested by study of Self-transcendence by the psychological profession?*
  3. *We need to research in greater depth* **where Spirituality reacts with the Physical Dimension in other areas than the Bible Code** *(such as the Psi factor, and the psychology of Faith).*
  4. *We need to know about* **the actual genes that give rise to Self-transcendence.**
  5. *We now know that God, the Supermind, does exist.* **Is there also a Sub-mind (= Satan)?** *If so, we need to know more about him?*
  6. *Does Science have a "blind spot" in its search for knowledge?*
  7. *If Man did undergo a Second Mutation in the Garden of Eden, how long would this take to be recognisable by science and how long to permeate mankind?*

To help to finance this research, the Author intends that a very large part of any profit due to him from the publishing of this book will be diverted to a **Spirituality Research Fund** *to be managed by either a suitable existing Charitable Institution, or by an Institute which he will initiate for the purpose.*

The sponsors of any Institutions feeling they might be able to provide sponsorship for such research and so provide the requirements of this Fund are invited to contact the author of this Easy Guide, via his publishing agent.

APPENDIX A

Results of Research undertaken by Thomas Wright into Comparison between Equidistant Letter Sequences (ELSs) of word lengths from 4 to "over 8" letters encoded into an original working version of the first five books of the Bible, Genesis, Exodus, Leviticus, Numbers and Deuteronomy (i.e. the Hebrew Torah), and a randomised version of the same.

Since the randomisation would have thrown a "Chance" selection of numbers of each letter-length, and a "Chance" selection will always be the same, subject to the Laws of Statistics, the results of these trials prove that the grand total of ELSs contained in the published version of the Torah could never have been produced by "Chance".

Two professional statisticians have vetted these figures, their method of selection and the conclusions drawn from the results.

Sample of 4-letter ELSs

Bible Story in which found	English word or phrase	Hebrew word as in Published text of Torah and transliteration	Number of times ELS occurs in Control Text for Torah (all "Chance")	Number of different times ELS occurs in Published version of Torah	Difference between Control and Published version	Difference between Control and Published as percentage of Published
Garden of Eden	Barley	שערה SheTzeRaH	110885	106044	-4841	-4.57%
Franz- of Austria	Franz	פרנץ FRaNTz	17380	17345	-5	-0.03%
	Joseph	יוסף YOSeF	30541	32278	1737	5.38%
Diabetes Story	Diabetes	סכרת SuKeReT	25751	23497	-2254	-9.59%
	Panchreas	לבלב LaVLaV	447107	422500	-24607	-5.82%
AIDS	Aids	איDס AIDS	39431	38848	-585	-1.51%
	Annihilation	מחיה MeChYaH	573256	570639	-2817	-0.46%
	Destroyed	הרהס HaRHaS	389677	380022	-9655	-2.54%
Murder of Pres- -ident	A murderer	רוצח ROTzeaCh	56967	53816	-2151	-4.00%
Sadat of Egypt	The consp- -iracy	הקשר HaKaSheR	133373	142695	9322	6.53%
	by the hand of	עליד ALYaD	192536	186296	-6240	-3.35%
	parade	מצעד MiTzAD	77943	74642	-3301	-4.42%
Totals			181680	155467	-6193	Av. %age 2.03%

Average percentage that 4-letter ELSs occur ABOVE CHANCE LEVEL in version of Torah first communicated by the composer to the Hebrews at around 1500BC:-   **-2.03%**

****

Sample of 5-letter ELSs

Bible Story in which found	English word or phrase	Hebrew word as in Published text of Torah and transliteration	Number of times ELS occurs in Control Text for Torah (all "Chance")	Number of different times ELS occurs in Published version of Torah	Difference between Control and Published version	Difference between Control and Published as percentage of Published
Story of Abraham	Abraham	אברהמ ABRaHaM	50538	49072	-1466	-2.99%
Story of Abraham	Fostov his birthplace	פסטוב FoSTOV	6	92	86	93.48%
Holocaust	by hands of SS	בידסס B'YaDSS	116	107	-9	-8.41%
	Eichmann	איחמנ EYChMaN	32002	30043	1959	-6.52%
	Hitler	היתלר HYTLeR	5479	6290	811	12.89%
	Berlin	ברלינ BeRLYN	24867	23951	-936	-3.91%
1st Gulf War	Sadam	צאדאמ TsADAM	643	561	-82	-14.62%
	SCUDB (missile used)	סקאדב SCUDB	375	485	110	22.68%
	3rd of Shevat (Hebrew day/mth first missile fired)	גבשבת 3B'SheVaT	134	136	2	1.47%
	Scud (missile)	סקדימ SCuDYM	485	375	-110	-29.33%
	Mt. Pisgah	הפסגה H'PiSGaH	122	138	14	10.29%
Devt. of Science/ Technology	Gravity	משיכה MaShUKHa	36951	33801	-3150	-9.32%
Totals			161680	155487	-6193	Av.%age 5.49%

Average percentage that 5-letter ELSs occur ABOVE CHANCE LEVEL in version of Torah first communicated by the composer to the Hebrews at around 1500BC:-   5.49%

****

Sample of 6-letter ELSs

Bible Story in which found	English word or phrase	Hebrew word as in Published text of Torah and transliteration	Number of times ELS occurs in Control (all "Chance")	Number of different times ELS occurs in Published version of Torah	Difference between Control and Published version	Difference between Control an Published a percentage of Publishe
Murder Of Pres. Sadat	Oct 6th (=8th Tishri) (Hebr.mnth)	חבטשרי 8th TIShRY	9948	10530	582	5.53%
Diabetes	Ketones	קתונימ KeTONYM	60	294	234	79.59%
	Naunyn (name of researcher)	נאונינ NAUNYN	3041	2930	-111	-3.79%
AIDS	the Immunity	החיסונ HaChYSUN	107	132	25	18.94%
Sadat Murder	Sadat	בסאדאת B'SADAT	54	65	11	16.92%
1st Gulf War	America	אמריקה AMeRYKHa	1142	1140	-2	-0.18%
About Civilisation (Predictions)	Shakespeare	שקספיר ShaKSPYR	3	19	16	84.21%
	Airplane (First flight)	אוירונ AUYRUN	4719	4357	-362	-8.31%
	Newton	ניותונ NYUTUN	241	28	43	15.14%
	He overturned present reality	הויהפח HUYaHePeK	2404	2345	-59	-2.52%
	Swift (name of comet)	סוויפט SWWYFT	9	9	0	0.00%
	Edison (electricity)	אדיסונ EDYSON	104	117	13	11.11%
Totals			11890	11784	-106	Av.%age 18.05

Average percentage that 6-letter ELSs occur ABOVE CHANCE LEVEL in version of Torah first communicated by the composer to the Hebrews at around 1500BC:- 18.05%

****

Sample of 7-letter ELSs

Bible Story in which found	English word or phrase	Hebrew word as in Published text of Torah and transliteration	Number of times ELS occurs in Control Text for Torah (all "Chance")	Number of different times ELS occurs in Published version of Torah	Difference between Control and Published version	Difference between Control and Published as percentage of Published
Aids	from apes	מהכופים MeHaKUFYM	36	32	-4	-12.50%
Frans-Joseph	Jerusalem	ירושלים YeRUSaLYM	297	280	-17	-6.07%
Sadat	Name of his murderer	אסלמבלו ISLaMBuLY	11	15	4	26.67%
1st Gulf War	Schwartz-kopf	שורצקופ ShVaRTzKOF	1	2	1	50.00%
	Fire on 3rd Shevat (Scud)	אשבגשבת ASheBGSheBaT	0	1	1	100.00%
Predictions of future civilisation	Watergate (re Nixon)	ווטרגיט WATeRGAT	0	1	1	100.00%
	Man-on-Moon	אישבירה AYShBYRaH	51	43	-8	-18.60%
	WrightBros (first fliers)	אחימריט AKYMRYT	7	13	6	46.15%
	1/3 of my people	שלישעמי Sh'LYShAMY	86	96	10	10.42%
	Nazi & Enemy	נאצויצר NATzYUTzeR	10	7	-3	-42.86%
	Autobus	אוטובוס AUTOBUS	3	5	2	40.00%
	Clinton	קלינתון KLYNTON	0	4	4	100.00%
Totals			502	499	6	Av% 32.77

Average percentage that 7-letter ELSs occur ABOVE CHANCE LEVEL in version of Torah first communicated by the composer to the Hebrews at around 1500BC:-

32.77%

****

Sample of 8-letter ELSs

Bible Story in which found	English word or phrase	Hebrew word as in Published text of Torah and transliteration	Number of times ELS occurs in Control Text for Torah (all "Chance")	Number of different times ELS occurs in Published version of Torah	Difference between Control and Published version	Difference between Control and Published percentage of Published
Assassination of President Rabin of Israel 1995	Yitzhak Rabin	יצהקרבינ YiTzaHKRaBYN	0	1	1	100.00%
Predictions of present day events	Schumaker-Levy (comet)	שומחרליו ShUMaKeRLeVY	2	3	1	33.33%
1st Gulf War	Lybian Artillary	תותחלובי TUTeKLUBY	8	10	2	20.00%
1930's Depression	Economic Collapse	שברכלכלי SheBReKLeKLY	1	1	0	0.00%
Predicted Developments	They prophesied a brainy person	נבאובמחנ NeBAYBeMCheN	1	3	2	66.67%
	Atomic Artillarymen	רגמאתומי RaGMATUMY	1	1	0	0.00%
	World War	מלחמתעלמ MaLKeMTALeM	1	1	0	0.00%
	A great People	לגויגדול L'GOYGaDOL	0	8	8	100.00%
	Oklahoma	אוקלהומה AUKLaHOMaH	7	11	4	36.36%
	Communism	קומוניזמ KOMUNYZM	0	1	1	100.00%
	Dynosaur	דינוסאור DYNOSAUR	0	1	1	100.00%
	9th AV 5756 (=July 25 1995) date of predicted death, but "delayed")	טאבהתשנו 9 AV 5756	1	1	0	0.00%
Totals			22	42	2	Av%age 46.36%^

Average percentage that 8-letter ELSs occur ABOVE CHANCE LEVEL in version of Torah first communicated by the composer to the Hebrews at around 1500BC:- 46.36%

****

Sample of "over 8-letter" ELSs

Bible Story in which found	English word or phrase	Hebrew word as in Published text of Torah and transliteration	Number of times ELS occurs in Control Text for Torah (all "Chance")	Number of different times ELS occurs in Published version of Torah	Difference between Control and Published version	Difference between Control and Published as percentage of Published
Aids	in the form of virus (10-letters)	בדמותוירוס B'DiMUTVYRUS	0	6	6	100.00%
	the end of all diseases (9-letters)	הקץלמחלות HaKeTz-L'MaChaLOT	0	1	1	100.00%
Frans Joseph	King of Austria (9-letters)	מלכאוסטרי MeLChAUSTRY	0	1	1	100.00%
predictions (various)	the next war (9-Letters)	מלחמההבאה MaLeKaMHaHaBAHa	0	1	1	100.00%
	Holocaust of Israel (9-letters)	שואתישראל ShUATYSRAyL	0	1	1	100.00%
	Assassin will Assassinate (11-letters)	רוצכאשרירצח RUTzKAeShRYRTzaK	0	1	1	100.00%
	Who is he? - President but he was kicked out. (16-letters)	מהואנשיאביתאבלגרש MeHYNShYAeBYTABLaGeReSh	0	1	1	100.00%
Science	Einstein (9-letters)	איינסתיינ AYYNShTYYN	0	1	1	100.00%
World War II	He (Hitler) was a mighty hunter before the Lord (13 letters)	הואהיהגברצידל HUAHaYaHGiBoRTzaYaDL	0	1	1	100.00%
Atomic Holocaust		שואהאתומית ShUAHATOMYT (10 letters)	0	1	1	100.00%
	His name is Timothy (9-letters)	שמוטימותי SeMUTYMOThY	0	1	1	100.00%
	fire, earthquake struck Japan (10 letters)	אשרערהכיפנ ASRARaHaKYaPaN	0	1	1	100.00%
			0	12	12	Av%age 100.00%

Average percentage that "above 8"-letter ELSs occur ABOVE CHANCE LEVEL in version of Torah first communicated by the composer to the Hebrews at around 1500BC:- **100.00%**

****

14.5   Summary and conclusions

All of these Hebrew-worded ELSs were selected entirely at random.

We have reached a point, therefore, where the proportions of selected ELSs that were <u>not</u> the result of Chance in the version of the Torah composed for the Children of Israel 3500 years ago, were as follows:

Category of ELS (by letter-length)	%age NOT "by Chance"
" 9(+) letters	100.00%
" 8 letters	46.36%
" 7 letters	32.77%
" 6 letters	18.65%
" 5 letters	5.49%
" 4 letters	-2.03%

[The small percentage (but of a large starting number) of minus figures for the 4-letter ELSs would be due to the longer ELSs in the published Torah having been converted to a larger number of shorter ELSs in the randomisation process to produce the scrambled version. It is noted that these figures show the <u>net</u> increase on a Chance figure; they take into account those Chance ELSs that were reduced in number, by having been dispersed in order to provide letters for the new inserted ELSs.]

These results of what, in all conceivable aspects, has been a fair comparison show that the percentage of ELS's in the original published Torah, as handed to the Children of Israel in around 1500BC, and as set out above, were not produced by Chance.

[Since these figures were downloaded from the Codefinder software around 12 months ago, I have taken every possible step I can think of to find fault with them. I must admit to having been slightly unnerved on finding that over this period, two ELS figures changed their reading. But these changes were not large enough to make any impact on the significance of the final Summary figures, above, or on the conclusions that have been drawn from them. In the end I concluded that this unexpected change in these two figures probably resulted from the following sequence of events:
(1) If the two versions of the Torah used for (a) the published and (b) the randomised control had been printed on paper, they would not have been expected to change at all over time.
(2) I can see, though, that over a period, the vibrations to which my lap-top was inevitably subjected, together with any possible wave bombardment that it might have been subjected to, could have disturbed either text on disc, to the extent experienced.
(3) Because of the unalterable behaviour of the products of Chance, one would expect that over a period, any vibrations tending to change the mix of numbers of ELSs would be equalised in both directions, so that the mix of sizes would for practical purposes remain constant.
This experience is mentioned here, since anyone checking my results could well have this same experience, and be puzzled by it.]

APPENDIX B
A BIRD'S EYE VIEW OF THE SCIENTIFIC PROOF OF GOD
1. Present position on knowledge of God

We are Scientists. We know so much that we nearly know it all. We can't find God, so must conclude that he just doesn't exist. There is no God -
We just know.

We are Believers. We just know he is there. We don't need Scientific Proof. We just know by Faith that God is there
We just know.

We are just Ordinary People. We just do not know at all.

2. What is Science?

(1) Science is the name given to the knowledge system invented by humans, in which has all been measured mathematically. New scientific knowledge is acquired by subjecting existing knowledge to calculation.
All scientific knowledge therefore can, by definition, be measured mathematically, and is proven to be correct.

(2) Knowledge that cannot be measured is not science.

(3) But Man is only able to measure by using one of his Physical Senses of sight, hearing, touch, taste and smell.

(4) So what is not measurable, such as colour, beauty, love, hate and spirituality, cannot become scientific knowledge.

(5) Science, therefore, is blind to Spirituality

3. What is Spirituality?

Spirituality is a Dimension of the Universe which extends alongside the Physical Dimension, but is quite separate from it. The Spirituality Dimension is different from, and does not obey the rules of the Physical Dimension, such as Gravity, Speed of light and Speed of Sound.

Examples of Spirituality are:-
  Spiritual Healing
  Ability to predict the future
  Metal Bending by the mind without the use of Physical
  force
  Unusual insight into the unknown
  Happenings that cannot be measured by physical means
  Religious happenings and experiences

4. Proof of the existence of Spirituality

There are a few areas of happenings which could only come from the Spirituality Dimension which react with the Physical Dimension to produce effects that can be measured, and therefore are proven scientifically.

These instances prove beyond doubt that the Spirituality Dimension does exist.

These areas are:-

Psi experiments - Telepathy (communication between minds without the use of the physical senses)
- Clairvoyance (the mind being able to "see" physical events without the use of physical sight.
- Psycho-kinesis (the ability to influence the movement of matter independently of physical force)

Masses of scientific experiments, using hidden cards and dice were carried out by and under the control of <u>Professor J.B.Rhine of Duke University</u> and are recorded in his book, <u>"The Reach of the mind" (1948)</u>.

Self-transcendence - a recently discovered Characteristic in the Temperament and Character Inventory (TCI) of some human beings, which enables them to live "outside themselves" for periods. These people are more receptive to religious teaching; but Self-transcedence is not itself a religion. Religion has to be taught; Self-transcendence is shown by twin-tests to be inherited. The relevant genes probably originated from mutation in a recent millennium

See book <u>"The God Gene" by Dean Hamer + research by Cloninger of Washington Medical School (around 2004)</u>
The Torah/Bible Code - masses of accurate and detailed predictions, of events happening in the 20th and 21st centuries AD, encoded into the First Five Books of the Hebrew/Christian Bible composed Bible 3,500 years ago.
(see <u>"The Truth of the Bible code" by Satinover (1997)</u>, <u>"The Bible Code" by Drosnin</u> and <u>my two current books for proof these composed by God</u>)

5. The Torah/Bible Code proves that a God does exist in the Universe

The Torah is encoded via the Equidistant Letter Sequence (ELS) system.......
an example:
Surface Text: I can do Vera and Lee a favor
Eliminate word spaces: I caNdoVerAanDleEafavor
Encoded ELS word: I N V A D E
It is generally agreed that humans have never had this degree of encoding or prediction capability. There are, therefore, only 2 possible sources of such

encodings:
(1) The falling by Chance, of the letters of the Surface Text: all texts have some ELS Chance encoding.
My two current books prove this to be impossible.
(2) Insertion by a Supermind of the nature of a God.
This, therefore is the only possibility.

IT IS THUS PROVEN THAT THERE IS A GOD IN THE UNIVERSE

This evidence also proves, incidently, that God personally composed the Torah. It also indicates that, God being a God of Truth, the Torah is a true historical account of the Creation.

A RECONCILIATION OF THE SCIENTIFIC AND BIBLICAL VERSIONS OF THE TORAH show that if allowance is made for God having to use "figure of speech" simplifications (e.g: as we do when we say "in the day of the Romans") to get the story understood by the iron-age Hebrews (only able to think in days, rather than long periods of years). There is only one major unexplained difference - the story of Adam and Eve (Garden of Eden). The most likely explanation of this is that it was a Second Mutation of Man, from Biological Man to Spiritual Man, able to communicate with the Spiritual Dimension ("in God's own Image"), around 4000BC. Starting with only one Man, it might not yet have produced enough evidence to be recognised by Science.

A SWOT Strategic Analysis of God's likely management position up to 4000BC, shows that God would have needed at 4000BC to initiate a Mutation of Man and to have initiated a religion-based training programme for Man. The Bible tells us that this is exactly what he did.

6. God in a Nutshell (as seen by Science)

(1) There is sufficient Scientific evidence from work on:
   (i) The operation of (a) Telepathy
                      (b) Clairvoyance
                      (c) Psycho-kinesis
  (2) Self-transcendence
  (3) The Bible Code
- to prove that a Spirituality Dimension exists.

(2) The Bible Code could only exist in either Dimension if an independent Supermind of the type associated with God had inserted it into the Bible.

THIS PROVES THAT A GOD EXISTS

7. The Need for further Research
(1) The evidence also points to there being two types of Man living at present in our World. We need positive proof of whether this is so, or not.
(2) We need confirmation of the truth of the Garden of Eden Story told in Genesis. One route to this could be via an analysis of the likely source and timing of the genetic mutation that introduced Man's Self-transcendence capability, through analysis of the present distribution of its sorld-wide distribution.
(3) The only source of information I could find of the estimated historical dates of happenings of the Old Testament period were those made by churchmen in the early 18th century, before these were over-ridden by scientifically proven dates. These need to be updated.

INDEX

Aaron 58
Abraham 55-6, 67
Adam 23, 35, 38, 53, 76
agricultural management 34, 36
Agricultural Training Board 32
Aids 42, 48, 62, 66, 68, 69, 71
Atheism 5, 8
HMS Atherstone (destroyer) 10

Bible Code
    challenge to iv, 2, 37, 40, 44-6, 63
  discovery of 25, 39, 40, 42
  evidence for iv, 1-2, 28, 32
  research team 2, 44-5, 46
  source of 4, 32, 37, 40, 44-5, 62, 63
    system of see ELS
    translation of 38
Big Bang theory 21
Bletchley Park 15
Brown, Rev. John 50
HMS Byron 15

Catechisms 6
chance 44-8, 52, 62, 65, 72, 75-6
Cipher Text 62
clairvoyance iii, 1, 25, 27, 36, 38, 61, 75
Cloninger, Robert 25, 28, 39, 62, 75
Codefinder software 72
communism 70
computers 42, 44, 58
Creation
  biblical theory of 41, 49, 63, 64
    scientific theory of 3, 7, 39, 49, 63, 64
  time span of 50
  two-tier 20-1, 23, 38, 49, 51, 76

D-Day landings 15
HMS Dakins (frigate) 15
determinism 7-8
diabetes 42, 48, 62, 66, 68
dinosaurs 70
Dixon (née Pinckert), Jeane 26
Drosnin, Michael iv, 75
Drucker, Peter 34
Duke University (USA) 27, 31, 36, 75

Eden, Garden of
  and creation 23, 35, 41, 49, 76
  foodstuffs grown in 44, 51-2, 62, 66
Edison, Thomas 68
Egypt 49, 53, 55, 57-9
Eichmann, Adolf 67
Einstein, Albert 28, 42, 48, 61, 71
ELS (Equidistant Letter Sequences)
  and chance 44-8, 52, 62, 65, 72, 75-6
  methodology of 42-3, 66-71
Enigma code 15, 42, 44
Esau 55, 56
ESP (Extra-Sensory Perception) 38
Eve 35, 38, 76
evolution 21, 23, 51
'external environment' 35

faith
  belief through 29-30, 73
  and doubt 3, 16, 20
  elusiveness of iii, 4,

Geller, Uri 26, 61
genes 25, 28, 64
God
  absolute power of 3, 20, 31, 35
  communication with 23

79

composes Torah 4, 38, 41, 45, 48, 49, 58, 62, 76
as Creator 3, 20-1, 31, 39
disillusionment with 5
hands Torah to Moses 41, 48, 58
inaction of 3, 8, 19
as manager 3, 20, 22-3, 31, 35, 39
personality of 20, 30-1, 35
role in the universe 20, 30, 35
and role of man 3, 20, 39, 51
in Spirituality dimension iii-iv, 25, 33, 41
strategy of 22-3, 31
supermind of 2, 32, 37, 39-40, 45, 49, 62-4
use of metaphor 38, 49-50, 76
gravity 67
great depression 70
Gulf War 42, 62, 67, 68, 69, 70

Hamer, Dean 75
Harvard University 34
Hebrews
    exodus of 53, 58, 60
    as God's chosen people 23
    nation of 55-60
    and the Torah 38, 41, 45, 48, 49, 62, 63
Hitler, Adolf 67, 71
Hitler Youth movement 6
Holocaust 42, 62, 67, 71
Homo Sapiens 21, 23, 51
Hurkos, Peter 26
Hussein, Saddam 67

Industrial Training Act (1964) 32
Institute of Spirituality 64
'internal environment' 35
Ipswich Further Education Institute 36
Irving, David 9-10
Isaac 55, 56
Ishmael 55, 56

Jacob 55, 56
Jesus Christ 23, 56
Joseph 55-7
Joseph, Franz 66, 69, 71

Koran 56

Lend-Lease Agreement (1941) 15, 34

mathematical measurement 30, 74
Mohammad, Prophet 56
Montgomery, General Bernard 10
moon landings 69
Moses 41, 48, 49, 53, 56, 58-60
mutation 20-1, 23, 38, 49, 51, 53, 62-4, 76-7
mysticism 28, 61

Near-Death experiences (NDE) 11
Newton, Isaac 68
Nixon, President Richard 69
Noah 49, 53-4

Pacific Western University (USA) 36
paranormal phenomena
    evidence of 25, 26, 61
    measurement of 4, 27, 39, 75
parapsychology 1, 4, 27, 39, 61, 75
Pearl Harbour 9
prayer 5
PSI factor 61, 75
psychic detectives 1, 26, 61
psycho-kinesis (PK) iii, 1, 25, 27, 36, 38, 61, 75

R101 (airship) disaster 26

Reading University 7, 9
Rebecca 55
religion 1, 5-6, 19, 29, 75
Rhine, Dr J.B. 27, 31, 36-7, 75
Rommel, Field Marshal Erwin 10
Roosevelt, President Franklin D. 26

Sadat, President Anwar El 66, 68, 69
Santerini 53, 58, 63
Sarah 55
Satan 64
Satinover, Jeffrey iv, 75
science
    fallibility of 30
    and measurement iii, 2, 29-30, 38, 74
    and parapsychology 1, 27, 75
    replaces God 3, 8, 19
    revolutionises society 3, 7, 19
    and spirituality 30, 37, 38, 64, 74-5
    standards of 1, 7
scientific journals iii
SCUD missiles 67, 69
self-forgetfulness 28, 61
self-transcendence 1, 4, 25, 28, 39, 61-2, 64, 75
Shakespeare, William 68
Sinai, Mount 41, 58
Smith, Joseph 28, 61
spiritual healing 1, 26
Spiritual Man 21, 23, 28, 51, 63
spirituality dimension
    God within iii-iv, 25, 31, 33, 41
    proof of 1, 30, 32, 36-8, 74-5
spirituality gene 25, 28, 64
Statistical Science (journal) iv, 2, 37, 44, 45, 62
Stone of Scone 26, 61
Swift (comet) 68
SWOT analysis 23, 35, 76
Systematic Management 22, 34-6, 39

telepathy iii, 1, 25, 27, 36, 38, 61, 75
Temperament and Character Inventory (TCI) 1, 28, 75
Ten Commandments 6
The Bible Code (book) 75
The God Gene (book) 75
The Reach of the Mind (book) 31, 36, 75
The Scientific Proof of God (book) iii, 2, 32, 37, 44, 46, 63
The Truth of the Bible Code (book) 75
Torah
    composed by God 4, 38, 41, 45, 48, 49, 58, 62, 76
    encoded messages see Bible Code
    historical truth of 3, 20, 23, 41, 49, 50, 53, 58, 63, 76
    metaphors used 38, 49-50, 76
    predictions of 1, 4, 39, 41-4, 48, 62, 66-71
    preservation of 41, 58
Transpersonal Identification 28, 61
Treaty of Munich (1938) 6
twin-test research 1, 28, 62

U-boats 9, 15

'values' 35

Washington Medical School 25, 28, 39, 62, 75
Weissmandl, Rabbi Michael 42, 44, 58
HMS Woodcock (sloop) 15
World Bank 36

World War I 3, 5
World War II 6-7, 9, 34
WRNS (Women's Royal Naval Service) 3, 16
Wright, Hazel 3, 16, 17, 19, 20, 29, 33
Wright, Thomas
    atheism of 3, 5-9, 19
  career of 32-3, 34, 36
  confirmation of 6, 9-10
  de-registration of 9, 19
  as determinist 7
  early education of 5-6, 19
  experiences a 'Presence' 11-14
  and faith iii, 3, 16, 19, 29
  family of 33
  father of 5
  injured at sea 10-11
  joins Royal Navy 3, 19
  lives as a Christian 3, 11-12, 16, 20, 29
  marriage of 3, 16, 17, 19, 29
  military training of 7, 9
  mother of 5
  as Navigating Officer 15
  Near-Death Experience (NDE) of 11-14, 29
  PhD attained 36
  at Reading University 7, 9, 19
  search for proof of God
    begins 16, 20, 29-30
    planning of 19-23
    research for iv-v, 2, 31-2, 44, 46-8, 65-72, 77
    stages of 48
  serves on HMS Atherstone 10-14
  serves on HMS Byron 15
  serves on HMS Dakin 15
  and University Training Corps 9
Wright Brothers 42, 48, 68, 69

CPSIA information can be obtained at www.ICGtesting.com
Printed in the USA
LVOW111824220512

282826LV00025B/223/P